Church, State, and Public Policy

A Conference Sponsored by the American Enterprise Institute for Public Policy Research

Church, State, and Public Policy

The New Shape of the Church-State Debate

Edited by Jay Mechling

American Enterprise Institute for Public Policy Research
Washington, D.C.

Cover illustration by Karen Laub-Novak.

Library of Congress Cataloging in Publication Data

Main entry under title:

Church, state, and public policy.

    (AEI symposia ; 79F)
    1.   Church and state in the United States—Con-
gresses. I. Mechling, Jay, 1945–   II. American
Enterprise Institute for Public Policy Research.
III. Series: American Enterprise Institute for Public
Policy Research. AEI symposia ; 79F.
BR516.C5   322′.1′0973   79-17711
ISBN 0-8447-2159-X
ISBN 0-8447-2160-3 pbk.

AEI Symposia 79F

Printed in the United States of America

PARTICIPANTS

William Bentley Ball
Attorney
Harrisburg, Pennsylvania

Dr. Peter L. Berger
Co-Director
Mediating Structures Project
New York, New York

Dr. Francis J. Butler
U.S. Catholic Conference
Washington, D.C.

Father John A. Coleman, S.J.
Woodstock Theological Seminary
Washington, D.C.

Dr. James M. Dunn
Director, Christian Life Commission
Baptist General Convention of Texas
Dallas, Texas

Monsignor John Egan
Assistant to the President
University of Notre Dame

Professor Donald A. Erickson
Center for Research on Public Education
University of San Francisco

Rabbi Arthur Hertzberg
Temple Emmanu-el
Englewood, New Jersey

Milton Himmelfarb
American Jewish Committee
New York, New York

Dr. Albert Huegli
President
Valparaiso University

Ellen Idler
Research Assistant
Mediating Structures Project
New York, New York

Rev. Dean M. Kelley
Executive Director for Religion and Civil Liberties
National Council of Churches

Theodore M. Kerrine
Executive Director
Mediating Structures Project
New York, New York

Dr. Christa R. Klein
Auburn Seminary History Project
Union Theological Seminary

Professor Jay Mechling
Department of American Studies
University of California at Davis

Professor Richard Morgan
Department of Government and Legal Studies
Bowdoin College

Rev. Richard John Neuhaus
Co-Director
Mediating Structures Project
New York, New York

Rabbi James Rudin
American Jewish Committee
New York, New York

David Seeley
Director
Public Education Association
New York, New York

Peter Skerry
Research Assistant
Mediating Structures Project

Father Joseph Sullivan
Executive Director
Catholic Charities Diocese of Brooklyn

Dr. James Wood
Baptist Joint Committee on Public Affairs
Washington, D.C.

The conference was held in New York City on May 26 and 27, 1978.

CONTENTS

FOREWORD

This book is based upon a conference that set out to look for the "new shape" of church-state relations. To say that there is a new shape to the relationship between the institutions of religion and government assumes, correctly, that the subject itself is not new. In fact this book explores a tension that is both very old and very necessary. Especially in the modern era, the state aspires to an all-comprehending jurisdiction that inevitably runs into conflict with the claims of religion. Authentic religion, after all, must refer to a sovereignty that transcends the authority of the state. The resulting tension between religion and the state is a dynamic that should not be, and cannot be, resolved by a neat "geometrical" formula. In a democratic society where no one institution monopolizes legitimate authority, this tension will always be assuming a new shape in response to new circumstances.

The particular circumstances which shape church-state relations today are frequently alluded to in the papers and discussion contained in this book. The events of recent times make clear that the church-state question is far from settled: the continuing debate over the role of religion in restricting abortions; congressional investigation into "cults," following the mass suicide-murders in Jonestown, Guyana, and the legal controversies surrounding groups such as Mr. Moon's Unification Church; the efforts of the Internal Revenue Service to narrow the definition of tax exempt religious activities and to regulate church-related schools in order to enforce laws against racial discrimination; the Labor Department's proposal to bring parochial schools under its supervision of employment practices. The purpose of this book is not to resolve any of these specific points of tension. It is to examine the guiding assumptions by which these and many other controversies should be resolved, always recognizing that such resolutions are provisional.

The distinctive guiding assumption of this conference was that decisions on church-state relations should take full account of the role of "mediating structures" in public policy. As spelled out in our monograph *To Empower People,* by mediating structures we mean those institutions in contemporary society that stand between the individual's private life and the large institutions (megastructures) of the public sphere. Notable among them are the family, organized religion, voluntary associations, the neighborhood, and ethnic and racial subcultures. The reader will readily recognize that not all the participants in the conference agreed with our understanding of mediating structures or their place in public policy. What was agreed by all is that mediating structures, and religion in particular, must be given clearer consideration in the forming of legal and governmental theory and practice.

The conference was organized by the Mediating Structures Project, in New York City, which is codirected by the undersigned, sponsored by the American Enterprise Institute for Public Policy Research, and partially funded by a grant from the National Endowment for the Humanities. Our special thanks is extended to Dean Kelley for helping to organize the conference, to Theodore Kerrine and his assistant Tatiana Stoumen for expediting it smoothly, and to Elliott Wright for his editing of the lively report written by Jay Mechling.

PETER L. BERGER
RICHARD JOHN NEUHAUS

INTRODUCTION

Jay Mechling

Those who gathered at the brownstone at 170 East 64th Street, New York City, could judge the purpose of the two-day conference from its title, "The New Shape of the Church-State Debate and Its Impact on Public Policies and Values." What was less obvious was the nature of the project sponsoring the conference.

Mediating Structures and Public Policy is a project codirected by Peter L. Berger, the sociologist, and Richard John Neuhaus, theologian and senior editor of *Worldview,* the magazine of the Council on Religion and International Affairs. With each invitation to the conference, the project codirectors included a copy of their monograph, *To Empower People: The Role of Mediating Structures in Public Policy* published by the American Enterprise Institute for Public Policy Research in 1977, which gave both the frame and the focus to the conference.

The Berger-Neuhaus project is a response to the major crisis in late twentieth century American civilization. On a general level, the crisis arises out of the collision of the American democratic ethos with the accelerating modernity of its institutions and of its consciousness. More specifically, this crisis takes the form of "the dilemma of the welfare state," a tension, between a continuing desire for the services of the welfare state and a deep-set animus against the bureaucratic, liberty-threatening leviathan of government which the welfare state seems to spawn. The tension is actually a dialectic; neither contradictory tendency is expendable in American thought, according to Berger and Neuhaus, who want to preserve both liberty and modernity in the democratic experiment. They see their project as an opportunity to encourage public policy in that direction.

"Mediating structures," the project's core concept, are "those institutions standing between the individual in his private life and the large institutions of public life."[1] The mediation takes place in the gap between the megastructures of the public sphere (corporations, government, larger labor unions, and the like) and the private, "home" sphere, the modern

---

[1] Peter L. Berger and Richard John Neuhaus, *To Empower People: The Role of Mediating Structures in Public Policy* (Washington, D.C.: 1977), p. 2.

American's primary refuge from the public world. The essence of the modern crisis for the individual is the discontinuity between public megastructures, experienced as overwhelming and alienating, and the private world, experienced as anomic, so "grossly under-institutionalized" that home is poorly equipped to provide a foundation for personal identity. This identity crisis has a political dimension as well, "because the megastructures (notably the state) come to be devoid of personal meaning and are therefore viewed as unreal or even malignant."[2] At stake in this dual crisis is nothing less than the American experiment itself:

> Without institutionally reliable processes of mediation, the political order becomes detached from the values and realities of individual life. Deprived of its moral foundation, the political order is "delegitimated." When that happens, the political order must be secured by coercion rather than by consent. And when that happens, democracy disappears.[3]

Many institutions have traditionally performed the mediating function. Four were selected by Berger and Neuhaus for the focus of their work. These are the neighborhood, the family, the church, and the voluntary association. The research design is a sort of four-by-five grid, with panels in five public policy areas—health care, housing and zoning, welfare and social services, education and child care, and criminal justice—examining the role of the four mediating structures in those areas. The conference that this publication records began with the church as mediating structure and moved outward to touch upon the public policy areas of health care, welfare and social services, and education—each of which is deeply involved with the state.

Three basic propositions define the research agenda of the Berger-Neuhaus project. The first is analytical: "Mediating structures are essential for a vital democratic society." This proposition "assumes that mediating structures are the value-generating and value-maintaining agencies in society."[4] Propositions two and three are programmatic recommendations; namely, a *minimalist* position, "Public policy should protect and foster mediating structures," and a *maximalist* view, "Wherever possible, public policy should utilize mediating structures for the realization of social purpose."[5] A major objective of the project is to "test" propositions two and three in the five public policy areas. The testing is entrusted to five panels of scholars and expert researchers charged to investigate

---

[2] Ibid., p. 3.
[3] Ibid.
[4] Ibid., p. 6.
[5] Ibid.

whether the programmatic propositions withstand scrutiny and can be translated into specific public policy proposals. *Empowerment* is the pivotal theme and the basic criterion for assessing public policy recommendations. Berger and Neuhaus write:

> Our belief is that human beings, whoever they are, understand their own needs better than anyone else—in, say, 99 percent of all cases. The mediating structures under discussion . . . are the principal expressions of the real values and the real needs of people in our society. They are, for the most part, the people-sized institutions. Public policy should recognize, respect, and, where possible, empower those institutions.[6]

To Empower People includes tentative conclusions about policy issues touching upon each of the four mediating structures under study. Those conclusions pertaining to the church should be summarized here for the sake of the ensuing discourses. At the heart of the Berger-Neuhaus view of the church as a mediating structure is an assumption that within "the family, and between the family and the larger society, the church is the primary agent for bearing and transmitting the operative values of our society."[7] Even in the case of Americans who do not consider themselves religious, "the values that inform our public discourse are inseparably related to religious traditions."[8] In other words, religious values cut across both the public and private spheres of life, but Berger and Neuhaus resist the popular tendency to regard "public" and "government" as synonymous. They insist that the church and other mediating structures are also "public" institutions in that they connect the individual to the megastructures of the society, and because they provide meaning and value to the megastructures. To merit the designation "mediating structure"—that is, to perform the mediating function described earlier—an institution necessarily must be public.

Berger and Neuhaus treat the "wall of separation between church and state" as a myth missing the fundamental fact that, Januslike, the church faces both the public and the private spheres. They see nothing in the First Amendment to the U.S. Constitution to contradict the church's essential nature as a mediating structure. The "no establishment of religion" clause in their view, "should mean that no religious institution is favored by the state over other religious institutions," and the "free exercise" clause implies to the authors that "no one is forced to practice or profess any religion against his will."[9]

---

[6] Ibid., p. 7.
[7] Ibid., p. 30.
[8] Ibid., p. 32.
[9] Ibid., p. 29.

3

"When there is neither favoritism nor coercion by the state, there is no violation of the separation of church and state,"[10] according to *To Empower People.* The fears of separationists that the churches will take over the state are dismissed as unrealistic; the far greater danger is that the state will take over all but the most narrowly defined theological functions of the churches. If that were to happen, then there would be no alternative to the state's "monopoly on the generation and maintenance of values."[11] Precisely such a monopoly characterizes totalitarian societies.

Thus it is, for example, that one minimalist approach would oppose the "symbolic sterility" of public space—a state of affairs produced by accumulated court decisions removing Christmas trees from city halls, prayers from public schools, and other religious symbols from communal space. In the delicate balance between community rights and individual rights, communal rights to public meanings and symbols are losing ground. In fact, one modern tendency of American liberalism is its defense of private rights against mediating structures. Berger and Neuhaus insist that "nobody has a right to be unaffected by the social milieu of which he or she is a part."[12] And the social milieu of the United States is historically, irreversibly, religious.

One final point should be drawn from *To Empower People* in setting the stage for the church-state conference. This involves particularity and pluralism. Berger and Neuhaus repeatedly caution that all discriminations are not alike. "Discrimination is the essence of particularism and particularism is the essence of pluralism,"[13] they say. The authors support non-racist discretion when it comes to public policy decisions, say, on the rights of a nursing home to restrict its clientele to members of one religious or ethnic group. They support the right of private, often church-related, adoption agencies to invoke religious criteria in placing children. "Liberation," write Berger and Neuhaus, "is not escape from particularity but discovery of the particularity that fits."[14]

To Empower People, and especially the section on the church as mediating structure, provided a general orientation and a set of terms as participants prepared for the conference on "The New Shape of the Church–State Debate and Its Impact on Public Policies and Values." The monograph was our "shared text," so to speak; all four authors of the conference papers used it as a touchstone for agreement and disagreement. At the same time, *To Empower People* is tentative enough to have offered

---

10 Ibid.

11 Ibid., p. 30.

12 Ibid., p. 32.

13 Ibid., p. 12.

14 Ibid., p. 43.

only the launching pad for a conference exploring the contemporary shapes and trends in the church-state encounter. It was the tentative, provocative nature of the occasion that generated an array of expectations as we assembled on May 26, 1978.

Any person charged with the responsibility of writing a report of a conference faces choices in organizing and style, and the reader is entitled to at least a brief explanation of the choices I have made. The mechanics of the conference were simple, and I have attempted to transfer that simplicity into the structure of this report. Four papers, distributed to participants in advance, provided the basic content and points of reference. One choice would have been to divide this report into four sections, with a paper followed by the ensuing discussion. That, however, would be unfair to the facts. Not one author read his paper in full, or even in large part. Assuming that the participants had already read the texts, each author highlighted what he took to be the major point in his paper and, in every case, offered illustrative information not contained in the paper.

True to the conference format, I have grouped the four papers into part one of the report. I have included portions of the authors' summaries in part two, the discussion, because they contain observations and data not found in the papers themselves and because it was the summaries which provided the immediate issues of debate.

The papers are arranged in the order in which their authors made presentations. Conference speakers were the Rev. Dean M. Kelley, executive director for religious and civil liberties of the National Council of Churches; Father John A. Coleman, S.J., of Woodstock Theological Seminary, Washington, D.C.; William B. Ball, the Harrisburg, Pennsylvania, attorney personally involved in many landmark church-state litigations; and Professor Donald A. Erickson, Center for Research on Public Education at the University of San Francisco.

My re-creation of the discussion in part two relies on tape recordings of the entire conference made with the participants' knowledge and on my own detailed notes. While my task is to give a true account of the conversations, I have tampered with the realities of speech in give-and-take discourse. Sometimes, I have used economic paraphrases of long exhortations or exchanges. I have used quotation marks when the words belong to the speaker, but I have avoided ellipses even when I have combined different portions of a person's comments into a continuous quotation. I have been careful not to put my words, or another participant's words, into a person's mouth, and I hope my paraphrases do not misrepresent anyone's views. I naturally hope that everyone at the conference will find in these pages the same conference I saw and heard, though I take full responsibility for this account.

I have also chosen to sacrifice logical movement from point to point for the drama of details in part two. A part of the truth of the conference is that we were often confused, and we moved in diverse directions. There was not the logic and the cohesiveness of expository writing. With the help of the moderators, Peter Berger and Richard Neuhaus, we paused from time to time to get clearer perspectives on the issues at stake, so that the narrative of the two days should give the reader some sense of recurring themes, counterthemes, and variations. In my Summing Up, I try to make ordered sense out of a conversational pattern that constantly folded back upon itself.

In the discussion, I have not used the titles—"Rev.," "Dr.," "Msgr." Titles of respect and accomplishment are included in the List of Participants. Identifications relevant to participation in the conference are also noted in the listing and are not repeated in the narrative section.

I want to add that Peter Berger and Richard Neuhaus gave me great latitude in my task. They encouraged me to be as approving or as critical as I felt necessary. The participants understood that they would exert no editorial control over the final report. Only a very few comments had to be "off the record" because they involved pending litigations or guarantees of anonymity. I thank the participants for their agreement to open terms.

Finally, I extend my thanks to Ted Kerrine, executive director of the project on Mediating Structures and Public Policy, for orchestrating the conference so efficiently.

PART ONE

THE CONFERENCE PAPERS

Confronting the Danger
of the Moment

Dean M. Kelley

It is often a matter of survival to confront the danger of the moment. Wars are lost by armies fighting with the weapons and tactics of a previous war, and relationships between the churches and the governments in the United States suggest that battles are being fought against enemies no longer present.

As Peter Berger and Richard Neuhaus put it in their seminal monograph *To Empower People,* "The danger today is not that churches or any one church will take over the state. The much more real danger is that the state will take over the functions of the church, except for the most narrowly construed definition of religion limited to worship and religious instruction."[1]

Franklin H. Littell expressed a similar view on one of the few occasions he attended the Church-State Committee of the American Civil Liberties Union. He said that, instead of fighting tax exemption of churches, we ought to be doing everything possible to *strengthen* churches and other voluntary associations against a monopolistic, monolithic, pretotalitarian government.

In confronting the danger of the moment, we should not abandon defenses that may be needed another day. Yet, manning all of them may hinder the present struggle. Which of our old redoubts can be abandoned, and which are essential for the future? Our choice will depend, to a large degree, upon what we believe to be constant, and what ephemeral, in human nature and relations. In this paper, I will try to sort out such distinctions.

The theme of mediating structures is an attractive one.[2] Individuals have little influence on the massive structures of big government, big busi-

---

Mr. Kelley is executive director for religious liberty of the National Council of Churches.

[1] Peter L. Berger and Richard John Neuhaus, *To Empower People: The Role of Mediating Structures in Public Policy* (Washington, D.C.: American Enterprise Institute for Public Policy Research, 1977), p. 30.

[2] See chapters 2 and 3 of *Why Churches Should Not Pay Taxes* (New York: Harper & Row, 1977).

9

ness, big labor, big media, and the like. Without intermediate institutions that are more amenable to their will, individuals are as helpless as Lilliputians against Gargantua. A Gulliver is needed in between.

Churches are not just mediating structures, of course. They have other, more important, functions, from which they may be distracted by the obligations of "mediation." But in some circumstances, they properly become the voice for those who might not otherwise be heard, acting as a counterpoise to giants and a critic (though not a rival) of principalities and powers.

In this paper, I will examine the possibilities and perils of the churches' role as "mediating structures" in light of current thinking about the church-state relationship.

The Church-State Background

Twenty-five years ago, church-state relations were a subject of intellectual ferment. The Fund for the Republic held a historic seminar in 1958 on the subject. The seminar was organized by John Cogley, and speakers included John Courtney Murray, Robert Maynard Hutchins, Leo Pfeffer, Will Herberg, James Hastings Nichols, Stringfellow Barr, Abraham Joshua Heschel, Gustave Weigel, and Paul Tillich. Participants included Robert Drinan, Martin Marty, Paul Ramsey, Norman St. John-Stevas, Marc Tanenbaum, and many others. It set the pace for much that was to come.

In those days, the heads of denominations met twice a year in Washington, D.C., at a "church-state-consultation" convened by Oswald C. J. Hoffman, now preacher on the Lutheran Hour. Eugene Carson Blake, Roswell Barnes, Carl F. H. Henry, and other notable figures attended regularly. Blake's classic castigation of tax exemption of churches was first presented to that group.[3]

Even the Methodist Church made a three-year study of church-state relations, in which Robert F. Drinan, John Cogley, Neil McCluskey, Claude Welch, and Arthur Gilbert participated.

For some people "church-state relations" was and still is a thinly veiled code for "stop the Catholics," and for others (then mainly Catholics) it meant, "parochial schools are entitled to tax money." There was considerable polarization of the two views. Three writers of the period whose legal credentials were excellent were viewed with suspicion by the separationists because they were "soft on parochial schools." I refer to Wilber Katz (*Religion and American Constitutions,* 1964); Paul Kauper

---

[3] Published in *Christianity Today,* August 3, 1959.

(*Civil Liberties and the Constitution,* 1962), and Philip Kurland (*Religion and the Law,* 1961). The Department of Religious Liberty of the National Council of Churches in 1963 made a study of parochial school textbooks in science, mathematics, and languages, showing the extensive religious content in what Congress was calling "secular subjects."[4]

A year later, the Department of Religious Liberty published a pamphlet "Public Funds for Parochial Schools?" which set forth reasons why such funding would be unconstitutional, contrary to good public policy, and counterproductive for religion and religious education. Yet, that department was one of the first national agencies of official Protestantism to try to develop lists of Roman Catholic leaders across the country with whom friendly communications could be developed, so that in cases of local Protestant-Catholic conflict, there would be someone in the vicinity who could act as mediator.

In 1963, the U.S. Supreme Court outlawed prayer in the public schools, and some of us labored vigorously to bring Protestant leadership from opposition to support for that decision. When the first effort was made in the House of Representatives to amend the Constitution to reverse the Court, spokesmen for the National Council of Churches and the major Protestant denominations led the long list of public witnesses before the Judiciary Committee *opposing* any "tampering with the First Amendment." When the same issue arose again in the early 1970s, dozens of staff persons of Protestant agencies worked fulltime for thirty days to head off what they viewed as an appalling throwback to Protestant folk-piety.

In 1965, church-state issues were argued bitterly in the shaping of Great Society legislation. One church-state consortium in Washington attempted to get a clear delineation in the regulations of the Office of Economic Opportunity to prevent church agencies from receiving federal funds. We were chagrined to discover that what would ordinarily be viewed as education was treated as welfare when supplied by OEO programs, and thus could be channeled through church agencies.

A similar device was used in the historic Elementary and Secondary Education Act of 1965, which was ostensibly designed to benefit educationally deprived children, and thus was supposed to be exempt from church-state strictures that might otherwise apply. In an effort to find a compromise between advocates of aid to parochial schools and advocates of aid to public schools only, some of the erstwhile strict separationists urged a formula derived from the "child benefit" theory the U.S. Supreme Court had used in *Cochran* v. *Louisiana* and *Everson* v. *Board of Education* (cases involving, respectively, the loan of textbooks and transporta-

---

[4] *Harvard Education Review,* vol. 32, no. 3, Summer, 1962; *Phi Delta Kappan,* June 1962.

tion for pupils in other than public schools). This concept was accepted by the mainline Protestant bodies (including the Baptist Joint Committee on Public Affairs), but was rejected by the Jewish agencies, the Unitarians, and the American Civil Liberties Union. Leo Pfeffer of the American Jewish Congress characterized it as a serious defection from, if not betrayal of, strict separation of church and state.

This formula was accepted, without great enthusiasm, by the U.S. Catholic Conference and was written into the Elementary and Secondary Education Act. Repeated and ingenious efforts were made to break this unusual alliance between Protestants and Catholics—without which federal aid to education might not have come into existence, at least not without expending political capital the Johnson administration needed elsewhere in the Great Society. But the alliance on the church-state settlement held, and the legislation passed. Catholics proved not nearly as committed to the child-benefit concept as were the Protestants, and the U.S. Office of Education and state departments of education proved not committed to it at all—if they even understood it.[5]

In the late 1960s, when the U.S. Supreme Court finally decided a series of cases on tax aid to parochial schools, it took a position more stringent than some of the separationists had urged. Ironically, some of us who had been arguing for years that public funds for parochial schools were unconstitutional were vindicated by the Supreme Court after we had begun to be attracted to a more moderate position. I, for one, felt that the Supreme Court had gone too far in striking down tax credits for parents of children attending parochial schools—one of the few church-state decisions on which I have disagreed with the Court.[6]

"Subsidiarity"

Back in those days, there was a running battle between the strict separationists and the apostles of an esoteric scholastic concept called "sub-

---

[5] A blow-by-blow description of this historic struggle is found in Dean M. Kelley and George R. LaNoue, "The Church-State Settlement in the Federal Aid to Education Act," Robert Gianella, ed., *Religion and the Public Order* (Villanova, Pa.: Villanova University Press, 1966); in Kelley, "State Regulations of the Participation of Pupils of Private Schools in Title I of the Federal Aid to Education Act," *Journal of Church and State,* vol. 8, no. 3, Autumn, 1966; and in George R. LaNoue, "Church-State Problems in New Jersey," *Rutgers Law Review,* vol. 22, no. 2, Winter, 1968. The last-named reports, researched in thirteen New Jersey parochial schools receiving Elementary and Secondary Education Act benefits, showed that some of the main elements of the church-state settlement were not implemented and perhaps could not be.

[6] See Dean M. Kelley, "Tax Credits and the Tests of Establishment," *Christian Century,* October 17, 1973.

sidiarity," which insisted that it is improper for a higher authority to intervene in matters which lower authority is able to handle. This seemed a not unreasonable notion, but hardly one that was writ large on the fabric of the universe, as Thomists seemed to think (in the jurisprudence of the United States, for instance, they said that Congress had "preempted" certain areas from the states).

As applied to the church-state arena, this concept had two unusual aspects: (1) the "lower authority," in this instance, was the church or local communities served by the church and (2) the "higher authority" of government was not to stay out of it completely; it was to continue to provide money, but to let the lower authority spend it. To the separationists, this way of thinking seemed at best unpersuasive and at worst diabolical.

We fought it with the logic of "who pays the piper calls the tune"— a rubric at least as weighty as subsidiarity and perhaps more so.[7] We kept insisting that the only way to be one's own master is to spend one's own money. (We did not examine very closely the meaning of "one's own money.") One cannot be "independent" on someone else's money, particularly when that someone else is the government, purporting to represent all of us. When a subsidiary authority receives money drawn from all of us by taxation, we said, it cannot use that money for the benefit of only some of us. It cannot exclude any segment of society from the civil benefits to which they are entitled. The Queen's shilling will sooner or later be followed by the Queen.

Hurst Anderson, of American University, benignly assured us that in all his years in higher education, the government had paid for many things but never once tried to exercise control; it wanted only good higher education. We pointed to *Simkins* v. *Moses H. Cohn Memorial Hospital*[8] as evidence that once-private institutions accepting tax funds (in this case, Hill-Burton grants for construction) could be required to follow stipulations (nondiscrimination against black physicians) not in the original contract, but the warning was not heeded.

Today, the Department of Health, Education, and Welfare is enforcing a number of regulations on all institutions that have received federal funds: nondiscrimination in admissions and employment, coeducation throughout (including physical education), and others which recently led

---

[7] If the state may aid these religious schools, it may therefore regulate them. Many groups have sought aid from tax funds only to find that it carried political controls with it. Indeed, this Court has declared that "it is hardly lack of due process for the Government to regulate that which it subsidizes." Wickard v. Filburn (Justice Jackson, in Everson v. Board of Education, 330 U.S. 1).

[8] 323 F. 2d 959 (4th Cir. 1963).

Dallin H. Oaks, president of Brigham Young University,[9] to issue a formal rejection of some HEW regulations as incompatible with the Mormon religious obligations of his institution.

Evidence of the government's propensity to regulate is increasing, and it is not limited to the areas government finances, as may be seen in the following:

• continuing efforts by state departments of education to regularize, standardize, and secularize parochial schools (particularly Amish and fundamentalist): *Ohio* v. *Whisner* (47 Ohio State 2d 181 (1976)) and *Hinton* v. *Kentucky State Board of Education.*[10]

• efforts by the Equal Employment Opportunities Commission to require nondiscrimination in employment, even within churches: *McClure* v. *Salvation Army* (460 F. 2d 553 (5th Cir., 1972)) and Southeastern Baptist Seminary

• attempts by the National Labor Relations Board to assert jurisdiction over lay teachers in parochial schools of the Roman Catholic Church: *Grutka* v. *National Labor Relations Board, Caulfield* v. *Hirsch,* and *NLRB* v. *Catholic Bishop of Chicago and Diocese of South Bend-Ft. Wayne.*

These are but straws in an increasingly adverse wind, one that has blown some of us toward a slightly different tack from the strict-separationist years. We have perceived that the government is not the universal source of salvation—or even the sovereign solvent of all human problems—that it was once thought to be. On the contrary, like all bureaucracies, including ecclesiastical ones, government is expansionist, centralist, rationalist, and uniformalist, and it, rather than any religious (or nonreligious) organizations, poses the danger of the moment.

How Do Churches "Mediate"?

Our purpose here is to consider how churches and other religious organizations can function as "mediating structures" in the sense suggested by Berger and Neuhaus in *To Empower People*. Churches now embody and express the parochial "will" of their members in many ways, particularly through recreational and athletic events, dramas, concerts, liturgical festivals, culinary extravaganzas, and the like.

---

[9] Dallin H. Oaks is also editor of one of the more significant collections of church-state writings, *The Wall Between Church and State* (Chicago: University of Chicago Press, 1963).

[10] *Editor's note:* a trial court decision limited state regulation of religious schools.

They also function occasionally as vehicles of civil intervention—to get a nearby street paved or a traffic light installed, to improve public schools or sanitation services, to press for appointment of more judges or municipal officials of their own persuasion, to protest police brutality, to demand a crackdown on prostitution or street crimes, to intercede for prisoners in the local jail or for pensioners in the poor house, to demand better hospital services or recreational facilities for youth. They have occasionally demanded, and even obtained, the temporary elimination of political corruption (for example, the Rev. Charles Parkhurst's attack on Tammany Hall in 1894).

They also encounter other "mediating" structures in the process and occasionally jostle or joust with other parishes, the local newspaper or TV channel, the PTA, a labor union, the Masons, or the American Legion. A church may remonstrate, on behalf of its members, with the county medical society to get doctors to make more house calls or to provide better services to clinics in the poorer part of town. In like fashion it could urge the local bar association to provide better legal services to indigent offenders.

Churches can and do provide their members with credit unions, shopping cooperatives, nursery schools, day-care centers, clubs, meetings, bazaars, rummage sales, clambakes, barbecues, bean suppers, and courses in everything from basket weaving to yoga. When they enter the area of educational and social services, however, they become of particular interest to Berger and Neuhaus, for they are competing directly with a government which functions increasingly as the sole dispenser of such services. It should be noted, however, that there are many modes of effective mediation that do not involve setting up and operating schools, clinics, or day-care centers.

That is not to say it is inappropriate or improper for a church to set up such institutions under its own auspices—far from it. That is one way to mediate, but only one way. Another would be to influence the policies and practices of existing institutions, both private and public. Operating satellite institutions is a vast undertaking that can draw off a large portion of the energies available to a church, and it probably should be attempted only if existing institutions are totally inadequate or unacceptable.

If a church feels compelled to set up a school or halfway house, a home for the aged, or a shelter for unwed mothers, it will be in the strongest "mediating" position if it can do so with its own resources: mainly the voluntary contributions of members and friends. To become dependent upon government for tax funds is to give hostages to the "enemy." Berger and Neuhaus devote much of their thesis to appealing to government to respect the autonomy and pluralism of mediating structures that are financed by government. Government may stay its hand awhile, but the situation is inherently unstable, and sooner or later Justice Jackson's dictum, "It is hardly lack of due process for the Government to regulate that which it subsidizes," will hold sway.

There are some mechanisms by which churches may try to "have their cake and eat it too," maintaining their independence from government while relying upon governmental financing, through the purchase-of-services, through intervening quasi-private dispensers (such as the National Endowment for the Humanities or the National Institutes of Health), and through tax credits for patrons of private service institutions. Some may want to devote much of the discussion to exploring such devices for insulating churches from government while still permitting government money, the most "contaminating" element of all, to flow through. Exploring ways to perfect the insulation *without* that contaminating flow might prove more fruitful.

Rather than risk the gravitational force of the Jackson dictum, churches might do well to insist upon the right to autonomy of the institutions they finance themselves. Even that will not be easy, as the government feels a "responsibilty" to regulate and certify *all* social services, not just those it finances, and it has the power to do so if it chooses to exercise it. Thus, even eschewing governmental financing does not provide a complete safeguard.

The battles for and against church autonomy are being fought today. Efforts have been made by government to regulate curriculum content in parochial schools (*Ohio* v. *Whisner*) and to intervene in hiring practices and union organizing of employees of churches.

The Internal Revenue Service has issued a regulation requiring all church-related institutions that it considers "charitable" or "educational," rather than "religious" to file annual informational returns as their "secular counterparts" do, thereby linking church-related schools, hospitals, and homes more closely with their secular counterparts than with the churches that founded them. Churches are exempt from filing such returns, as are their "integrated auxiliaries," but apparently churches are not to determine what their integrated auxiliaries are; the government will do that, mainly on the basis of whether or not the auxiliaries are "religious."

Extraterritoriality

Some would strive for a sort of "extraterritoriality" for churches to keep government completely out of their affairs. That was the course Florence Flast and I urged in a recent debate in the Church-State Committee of the American Civil Liberties Union. We contended that the National Labor Relations Board should have no jurisdiction over the professional employees of Roman Catholic parochial schools. If such schools are too "religious" to receive tax funds, we said, they are religious enough not to be subject to governmental regulation—a view taken recently by the Seventh Circuit Court of Appeals in *NLRB* v. *Catholic Bishop of Chicago*.[11] We lost, six to two. The opponents of our view said that anything tending toward extraterritoriality was outrageous and that churches should not be exempted from general laws applying to others. The import of *Sherbert* v. *Verner* and *Wisconsin* v. *Yoder*[12] is not that churches should be outside the law" but that the First Amendment protects free exercise of religion at the point where a law actually interferes with a specific exercise of religion, and not before. Therefore, they said, the National Labor Relations Act should apply to employees of churches as to all other employees until an actual interference with religious practice occurs. Only then, and only to that extent, we were told, can the church claim relief, and then its interest must be weighed against other compelling interests of the republic.

James Madison, not understanding this view, wrote long ago: "It is proper to take alarm at the first experiment upon our liberties."[13] Otherwise, what is today but a "trickling stream" can become a "raging torrent."[14] Some would apparently wish he had written: "It is proper to take alarm only after government has experimented with our liberties, and then only if the experiment has really impaired them."

Hazards of Extraterritoriality

The problem with setting churches in a special enclave where government cannot touch them may be that they will become isolated from the civil life of the commonwealth, unaffected by it and unable to affect it. That would not be mediation but encystment. There are already pressures in that direction from those who maintain that "separation of church and state" should cut both ways; it should not only keep the government from interfering with churches but also keep churches from interfering with

---

[11] 559 F. 2d 1112 (1977).

[12] The former is the historic case in which the Supreme Court ruled that a woman cannot be denied unemployment compensation if she refused to work on Saturday because of religious scruples. In the latter, the Supreme Court said the state of Wisconsin did not have compelling reason to override Amish religious beliefs by requiring that Amish children go to public school beyond the eighth grade.

[13] James Madison, "Memorial and Remonstrance," quoted in Anson Phelps Stokes and Leo Pfeffer, *Church and State in the United States* (New York: Harper & Row, 1964), p. 56.

[14] Words used by the U.S. Supreme Court in conjunction with the foregoing quotation from Madison in Abington Township v. Schempp.

government. Indeed, the Internal Revenue Code, by threatening loss of tax exemption for "substantial" efforts to influence legislation, tends to keep churches and other exempt organizations out of the political arena.

Of course, the First Amendment prohibits Congress from enacting any law that would give churches official entree to the processes of government—for example, by designating certain prelates members of the Senate (as in England certain bishops of the established church are members of the House of Lords). But that is a far cry from churches and their members expressing their views to legislators and other officials. They have no more means to *compel* such officials to heed them than has anyone else, and certainly less than has the AFL-CIO.

The U.S. Supreme Court has recognized the right of churches to intervene (as a private group of citizens, not as an official body) in public affairs. The Chief Justice put it this way:

> Adherents of particular faiths and individual churches frequently take strong positions on public issues including, as this case reveals in the several briefs *amici,* vigorous advocacy of legal or constitutional positions. Of course, *churches,* as much as secular bodies and private citizens, *have that right.*[15]

It should not be gratuitously assumed that the absence or minimization of legal bonds and contacts between churches and governments will necessarily mean a severing of all other relationships as well. That could be the consequence, but it is less likely than the opposite: that fiscal relationships will increase regulatory ones. If we are to look realistically at the latter, let us do likewise with the former. Cheap shots at the concept of "separation of church and state" will not help us do either. Separation of church and state is no more an absolute than is separation of powers: they are both constitutional *ideals,* to be approximated as nearly as possible while respecting other important constitutional ideals. They are something we should strive to move *toward* rather than away from.

Churches can be vigorous and dynamic mediating structures in many informal and unofficial ways in their communities and regions, and in the nation as a whole, without relying on formal, official status, on governmental delegation of authority, or on governmental financing. In many ways, the churches would carry greater "clout" by appraising social services and helping other institutions (both public and private) than they would by being just another operator of institutions.

The Consumers' Union has gained its reputation as a *tester* of other people's products, not as a competing manufacturer. To avoid even the

---

[15] Walz v. Tax Commission, 397 U.S. 664 (1970). Emphasis added.

appearance of collusion, it refuses to accept gift samples of merchandise for testing, but buys its own samples at the open market price. What would happen to its reputation if the Consumers' Union became, not a disinterested tester of products, but a *promoter* of some, a client or agent of General Electric, for instance?

In the same sense, churches should be "testers" of social services, particularly governmental ones. They should neither be nor be seen as advance agents, clients, or "shills" for any governmental program or office. Thus, in my view, they should never be on any governmental payroll. Surely they could "help" lots of people in such programs, but is that the best kind of help churches can give? Sometimes people need advocates more than helpers.

A Few Parting Demurrers

As I have indicated elsewhere,[16] I believe churches have a high and demanding function consisting of religious ministrations: "explaining the meaning of life to their members in ultimate terms." I would not want to see that urgent function neglected for the sake of a secondary one—acting as a mediating structure. The two functions are not incompatible, indeed they may overlap in several areas, particularly in the supportive role of the believing community for its members, which makes the "meaning" function possible. But many churches have sold their religious birthright for a mess of social service pottage, and the result is that not even the poor turn to them for religious help.

The greatest help churches can give to their members, to the poor, and to society as a whole is not in the area of social service or education, but in the area of meaning. They should not neglect this function for the sake of social service, particularly not for the administering of conventional programs (which almost any other agency could administer as well or better) paid for with public funds, precluding the unique kind of religious ministry that makes such programs efficacious. Berger and Neuhaus, because of their desire for a new earnestness in, and respect for, the churches, should be precisely the people to warn them against the temptation to become the handmaiden of anyone but the Lord.

I agree with them thoroughly that the churches are not about to wither away in the glare of education and modernization, and that the churches do not deal solely with the private sphere of life but are very relevant to public policy. I disagree with their idea that the "no establish-

---

[16] Dean M. Kelley, *Why Conservative Churches are Growing* (New York: Harper & Row, 1972, 1977).

ment clause" permits state favoritism of one religious institution over others. The U.S. Supreme Court said in regard to this idea in 1963:

> [T]his Court has rejected unequivocally the contention that the Establishment Clause forbids only governmental preference of one religion over another. . . . Such contentions, in the light of the consistent interpretation in cases of this Court, seem entirely untenable and of value only as academic exercises.[17]

The Court has also referred to Philip Kurland's idea that religion should not be used as a classification in law either to confer a benefit or to impose a burden, but that it is not unconstitutional if a law having proper secular objectives incidentally benefits religion. The Court, however, has never adopted this idea.[18] Of course, the Court may change its views and disentangle itself from what Berger and Neuhaus view as the confusions into which it has been led, but I prefer its confusions to Kurland's spurious clarity or Berger and Neuhaus's reconstructions.

There are times when the First Amendment seems to afford benefits to religion, as in its granting of tax exemption and institutional chaplaincies, and other times when it seems to impose disadvantages, as in its denial of government subsidies, but to treat religion as though it did not exist is not a way to enhance its public standing.

I disagree vehemently with Berger and Neuhaus on the propriety of setting up religious symbols on public property. I agree that such symbols should not be privatized, but there are gradients between the opposing views. Between government property and private property there are "common" and "public" properties. The former are like "the commons" in a colonial town or a park in the village square, the latter would be various sites around the square, such as street corners and sidewalks, which the Supreme Court has characterized as "public thoroughfares," where any and all might express their views.

Placing the religious symbols of one religious faith-group, or of several, on the courthouse steps (the "governmental" area), would be like taking possession of the courthouse on behalf of that group or groups, at the expense of all others. The implication might not be as gross if the symbols were placed on the commons, still less on the public thoroughfare. In my opinion, they belong in none of those places; they belong on the property of the church, where they are more "public" than on a private residence and less "pushy" than on a village green.

I am not opposed to church-related institutions of social service receiving tax funds under a purchase-of-services sort of arrangement, or

---

[17] Abington Township v. Schempp, 374 U.S. 203 (1963).

[18] Philip Kurland, *Religion and the Law* (Chicago: Aldine Publishing Co., 1962).

educational institutions benefiting from tax credits available to patrons, or to a voucher program. But I am wary of a situation such as is said to exist in the Netherlands, where the society is divided into Catholic, Reformed, and re-Reformed "pillars" (or *verzuiling*), each with its own schools, hospitals, clubs, newspapers, unions, and so forth. Not only does such sectarian segmentation carry pluralism too far, but it can mean that a citizen who does not belong to one of the two or three favored religious groups in a community must go through an alien religious portal to gain his civic benefits. As hospitable as they may be, he is still a guest in someone else's house, when he ought to be as much at home in a common civic house as any other citizen.

A Theological Link between Religious Liberty and Mediating Structures

John A. Coleman, S.J.

John C. Bennett has said that "there is no one Protestant doctrine concerning church-state relations."[1] The best single historical-theological survey of varying Protestant theologies of church and state distinguishes five sharply divergent ideal-typical sets of doctrine. These range from the classic Lutheran two-kingdom concept with its stern, perhaps unbridgeable, division between law and gospel, through the Anabaptist disdain toward the state as an agency at best sub-Christian, or the Quaker perfectionist expectations for a pacifist liberal state, to the strict separationists for whom the guiding metaphor is "the wall," as opposed to the transformationists, who argue that "God has an intention for society as well as the church which the churches must mediate and make effective."[2]

A rounded theology of church-state relations demands close attention to such questions as:

• What is the nature of the church or the religious people? Is it a purely voluntary association of persons united for religious purposes, or does it represent an institution ordained by God? Who speaks for the church on public issues, and what authority and style is appropriate to this address?[3]

• What is the nature of the state? To what degree is it the result of sin; to what degree ordained by God? Are there permanent or accidental aspects of the state (war making, coercion, office holding, oath taking) inconsistent with Judaism or Christianity? How does the church handle such religious conflict? To what extent can the state be perfected to serve

Father Coleman is on the faculty of the Jesuit School of Theology, Berkeley, California.

[1] John C. Bennett, *Christians and the State* (New York: Charles Scribner's Sons, 1958), p. 205.

[2] Thomas C. Sanders, *Protestant Concepts of Church and State* (New York: Holt, Rinehart and Winston, 1964), p. 257.

[3] This question is raised in Paul Ramsey, *Who Speaks for the Church?* (Nashville: Abingdon, 1967), and James Gustafson, *Christian Ethics and Community* (Philadelphia: Pilgrim Press, 1971).

the purposes of the kingdom of God? What is the relationship between society and the state?

• To what degree must the church or its people be independent of the state? Is there a gradation in the forms of church-state relationship, some more in accord with Jewish or Christian concerns than others?

• Does the independence of church and state deny all relationship between the two? Is God sovereign over both? If so, in what forms does the sovereignty of God over the state manifest itself?

• What are the obligations toward the state of the church and of Christians and Jews, as citizens with dual loyalties? To what extent should the church support the aims of government? Is patriotism a Judeo-Christian virtue?

• With what means and under what conditions may Christians or Jews oppose a tyrannical or unjust government? What obligations, if any, does the state or society have toward the churches and the care of religion? Under what circumstances can a state restrain claims to religious freedom? Can the church legitimately demand concessions from the state? Under what circumstances can the church try to influence the state?

• How virtuous can a government be? How does Christianity or Judaism enhance this virtue? What is the role of order, peace, justice, welfare, and the care for societal freedom in God's intentions?

• What is the theological ground for asserting religious liberty or defending the nonestablishment clause of the First Amendment of the U.S. Constitution?[4]

Thomas Sanders contends that very few of these questions have attracted and sustained the attention of Protestant bodies with the exceptions of religious liberty, the nature of the church, and the religious base for social and political responsibility. He also claims that "the most minimal objective studies now taking place in the denominations reveal the obvious, that Protestants have functioned in this key area through misinformed anti-Catholicism and *legal* rather than *religious* norms."[5]

As this thicket of theological, ethical, political, and juridical issues suggests, one would not expect to find a definitive Protestant, Catholic, Jewish, or secularist position on church and state.[6] The complexity and variety of issues connected with determining a coherent church-state position foster plural outcomes. As the range of questions makes clear, it is difficult to conceive of separation as an absolute category.

---

[4] For these questions, see Sanders, *Protestant Concepts,* pp. 288–299.

[5] Ibid., p. 279.

[6] For a theocratic position with strong assertions about the rights of Judaism vis-à-vis the state, see Manfred Vogel, "Critical Reflections," in Walter Burghardt, ed., *Religious Freedom: 1965–1975* (New York: Paulist Press, 1977), pp. 54–69.

There is still no one Catholic position on all aspects of church and state. Writing at the time of the Second Vatican Council debate on the Declaration on Religious Liberty (*Dignitatis Humanae*), John Courtney Murray distinguished five positions within the Council.[7] One was the older Catholic view that error has no rights, that only one who is in the truth, therefore only a Catholic, has an intrinsic and natural right to religious freedom. Moreover, this stance claimed for the church a preeminent juridical position in civil societies as something demanded by theology and reason. As the vote on the declaration at the Council showed, this position was held by a decided, even minuscule, minority. And yet, as Monsignor Pietro Pavan—who with Murray was the principal architect and draftsman of *Dignitatis Humanae*—has recently argued, this understanding has emerged again in some sections of the postconciliar church.[8] It lacks, however, articulate spokesmen or suasive argument.

Among those who supported a declaration on religious freedom at the Council, some pleaded for a merely practical document, a declaration of pastoral policy rather than a statement of theological principle. They were countered by the argument that this might seem to be the work of opportunists, a dubious—please excuse my embarrassment at the consecrated term—jesuitical act of mental reservation. Still others wanted to ground the declaration upon the indubitable Catholic principle of the freedom of conscience. Proponents of the final declaration argued that this tack would not result in a rationally justified stance in favor of religious expression in the public order. The subjective rights of conscience could still be countered by objective claims to truth.

The Catholic theological positions on religious liberty that are still seriously competing are Murray's view, which carried the day at the Council, and a view largely associated with French theologians. John Courtney Murray contended that the case for religious liberty should rest on a complex religious-political-moral-juridical argument that appeals simultaneously to the exigencies of human dignity and the learning experiences of history. He demanded that the Council document include a statement about the juridical need to enshrine religious liberty as a civil right in a constitutional government of limited powers. Still competing with Murray is a position that tries to predicate religious freedom entirely on theological grounds. This position runs the risk of triumphalism and the patently false assertion that religious liberty is primarily a Christian invention. As George Linbeck has remarked about similar Protestant moves to substan-

---

[7] John Courtney Murray, "Religious Freedom," in John Courtney Murray, ed., *Freedom and Man* (New York: P. J. Kenedy and Sons, 1965).

[8] Pietro Pavan, "Ecumenism and Vatican II's Declaration on Religious Freedom," in Burghardt, *Religious Freedom,* pp. 32–33.

tiate religious liberty purely on particularist Christian theological premises, there is no way one can show, on these grounds alone, why reasonable persons who are not Christian should grant religious liberty to all.[9] Moreover, a purely theological argument for religious liberty does not lend itself to civil discussion in a broader secular context.

There has been very little Roman Catholic theological writing or discussion on religious liberty or separation of church and state since the adoption of *Dignitatis Humanae* and Murray's death. There has been, however, some new thought on the constitutional provisions of the First Amendment and on policy related to American governmental aid to religiously sponsored activities, such as schools and welfare organizations. In part this paucity of discussion is attributable to a prevailing sense that Murray's position has carried the day—the problem is solved, the question closed. In part it reflects the fact that in Catholic thought the more limited constitutional issue of church-state separation is subordinated to broader questions of church-society relationships, the proper mission of the church to modern society, and what "the signs of the times" tell the church about its role and appropriate evangelical style of ministry. These issues are raised in the Second Vatican Council document *Gaudium et Spes,* and after the Council by political theology in Europe and liberation theology in Latin America.[10]

Murray saw *Dignitatis Humanae* as the forerunner of *Gaudium et Spes.* Religious liberty set the church free to pursue social ministry in modern society. As he noted, "*Gaudium et Spes* is clear that the church's ministry is religious, not political in nature; yet the animating religious vision of the gospel has substantial political potential."[11] The general thrust of postconciliar Catholic thought has been to fight vigorously against narrow "churchy" conceptions of the religious task and the pervasive privatization of religion. Thus, for example, the 1971 Synod of World Bishops could assert, "Action on behalf of justice and participation in the transformation of the world fully appears to us as *a constitutive dimension of the preaching of the gospel,* or, in other words, of the church's mission for the redemption of the human race and its liberation from every oppressive situation."[12] This position contains a strong animus against any attempt

---

[9] George Linbeck, "Critical Reflections," in Burghardt, *Religious Freedom,* p. 54.

[10] The failure of this new theology to address the issue of the limited constitutional state is part of my criticism of liberation theology in "Vision and Praxis in American Theology," *Theological Studies,* vol. 37, no. 1 (March 1976), pp. 3–40.

[11] John Courtney Murray, "The Issue of Church and State at Vatican Council II," *Theological Studies,* vol. 27 (March 1966), pp. 599–600.

[12] Cited in David O'Brien and Thomas Shannon, eds., *Renewing the Earth: Catholic Documents on Peace, Justice and Liberation* (Garden City, N.J.: Doubleday, 1977), p. 391. Emphasis added.

to segregate the church from participation in formulating the moral aspects of political questions or to relegate it to the sacristy. The position places social service and social action, even that directed toward non-Catholics and nonbelievers, on an equal religious footing with preaching the gospel and administering pastoral care. We find in this view a twentieth century Catholic version of the earlier Calvinist sense of worldly calling. It is appropriate to note that the church's self-understanding spills over to its claims for the freedom in the public order necessary to fulfill its proper mission. Such a self-understanding will chafe at narrowly construed definitions of the public scope for the church in some interpretations of church-state separation.

Since the Council, the appropriate church response to the problems of modern society, or to liberation and development in the Third World, rather than the narrower questions of religious liberty or church-state separation, has been the dominant issue in Catholic social thought. It remains true, however, as James Rausch contends, "that the nature of the church-state relationship in a given political culture directly and significantly shapes the field within which the church can exercise prophetic witness in society" such that "the classical issue of church-state is an essential factor in determining how the contemporary issue of church-society takes concrete historical shape."[13] The key question here is, To what extent does an understanding of the separation of church and state promote or restrict the church's role as a mediating structure in society? What scope, beyond worship and catechesis, is allowed the church for action in education, welfare, health, the media, and the world of work and economics? The strategy and style of church influence upon culture and society have changed dramatically in the post-Vatican II era with the church's adoption of a new posture of dialogue and pluralistic participation. There is no evidence, however, that its ambitions toward influencing the morality and quality of public life have in any way diminished.

In our American context, new questions about church-state separation related to abortion laws, indirect aid to religious schools through vouchers, and the threat by the Internal Revenue Service to determine what constitutes "authentically religious" action not only raise anew the legal questions about the interpretation of the First Amendment. They also demand clarification of the theological and ethical presuppositions of that amendment in a pluralistic society.

It is as true today as it was two decades ago that one has to draw from the works of Murray, Jacques Maritain, Yves Simon, and H. A. Rommen

---

[13] James Rausch, "Dignitatis Humanae: the Unfinished Agenda," in Burghardt, *Religious Freedom,* pp. 40–41.

to articulate the Catholic case for disestablishment, religious liberty, the nature of the state and its distinction from society, and subsidiarity.[14] There have been no recent Catholic theoretical breakthroughs on these issues. With the adoption of *Dignitatis Humanae,* however, the thesis of these writers came into ascendancy in Catholic theology.[15] Theirs is, indisputably, the reigning paradigm among Catholic intellectuals and theologians.

I am going to draw upon the work of these authors, especially Murray, to rehearse briefly the dominant theological-ethical-juridical case for religious liberty, separation of church and state, and subsidiarity. I will indicate throughout how this case depends simultaneously on theological underpinnings and a secular warrant. Much of the Catholic brief for religious liberty is well known. I will highlight, however, a little noted aspect of the brief, namely the way Murray's structuring of the argument is dependent on a strong corollary case for mediating structures. At crucial points, Murray's argument for religious liberty subsumes a case for subsidiarity as the critical middle term of argument. It will be my contention that the freedom of the church flourishes best in societies with a vigorous structure of mediating associations. Moreover, in totalitarian societies, those churches with their own network of mediating structures are best able to withstand the state and assert effective freedom of the church. At various points I will add my voice to the policy debate on the role of mediating structures raised by Berger and Neuhaus's *To Empower People* and Kelley's "Confronting the Danger of the Moment."

The Importance of Secular Warrant in Theological Argument

It would be a mistake to see the Catholic case as an exclusively Catholic preserve. Of course, the Catholic argument on church-state relations has often been infected with particularist theological bias—more so than it has pretended in the past with its claims to speak for the natural law.

Catholic theories of the state have always relied upon reason—what the tradition called natural law but I prefer to call secular warrant—as well as revelation. Protestant, Jewish, and secularist disclaimers from the theory of natural law, basically three critiques, are well-known. First, it is

---

[14] See John Courtney Murray, *We Hold These Truths* (New York: Sheed and Ward, 1960) and *The Problem of Religious Freedom* (Westminster, Maryland: Newman Press, 1965); Jacques Maritain, *Man and the State* (Chicago: University of Chicago Press, 1951); Yves Simon, *The Philosophy of Democratic Government* (Chicago: University of Chicago Press, 1951); H. A. Rommen, *The State of Catholic Thought* (St. Louis: B. Herder and Co., 1945).

[15] References in this chapter are to the text of *Dignitatis Humanae* in O'Brien and Shannon, *Renewing the Earth,* pp. 291–306.

argued, largely by Protestants, that the Catholic appeal to secular warrant is not justified theologically because of the pervasiveness of sin, which distorts both human desires and reason. Only a basic certainty given in revelation, Protestants argue, can overcome sin's distortions of reason. Second, not all persons of intelligence and good will agree upon the neutral secular warrants alleged as self-evident and integral to the Catholic case. Finally, the substantive norms and principles developed by Catholic social thought often reflect the social and cultural conditions of the medieval period in which the theory developed.[16]

I want to summarize three shifts in the Catholic understanding of the usage of secular warrant in theological argument. The issue is important because critical elements of the Catholic position on church and state rest on secular warrant. The first shift is an explicitly theological understanding of the natural or secular as transformed in grace. The Protestant ethicist James Gustafson states this new theological understanding of nature:

> Persons know grace who do not know grace *as* grace; those who are acting in conformity with their true natures are acting in grace. Those who act morally are Christian; they are not to be thought of only as autonomous rational beings governing their conduct in accord with principles derived from the moral order of "nature" (in the sense of something distinguished from grace). Though anonymously so, they are Christian. Those who act morally are not only preserving the created moral order in the face of threats to it; they are participating in the order of redemption.[17]

As Gustafson further notes, this is a new Christian theological warrant for the possibility and necessity of dialogue between Christians, non-Christians, and nonbelievers. Its appeal is not so much to a putative residual order of autonomous nature untouched by sin (objectionable to classic Reformation thought as a species of Pelagianism) as to the universal ontological transformation of all persons by grace, whether or not they are Christian, whether or not they are conscious of the transformation. This understanding of natural law and the secular agrees fully with the classical Protestant insistence on the absolute necessity of the grace of Christ to overcome the pervasiveness of sin. It assumes, however, that the grace of Christ is available even to those who do not consciously accept the Christian revelation. The sacred claims for Christian grace are extended to include at least some secular experiences and warrants. The Reformation

---

[16] For these objections, see James Gustafson, *Protestant and Roman Catholic Ethics* (Chicago: University of Chicago Press, 1978), p. 62.

[17] Ibid., p. 118.

theologians asserted that all was either grace or sin. Catholics agree. Yet some grace is not consciously known as such. My purpose in dredging up this intramural Christian theological discussion is to show the possibility, on these grounds, for Christians to seek nonparticularist warrants for their moral stances. They can base parts of their theological reasoning not only on special revelation but also on a general revelation available to all. Their appeal, in short, is also based on secular warrant.

The second shift is the growing assumption that only when the secular warrants claimed in Catholic moral and social theory gain a wide ecumenical consensus among other Christians, Jews, and secularists is there any clear indication, even for Catholics, that the warrants are not unique conclusions surreptitiously derived from the Catholic tradition. This is not per se a consensual view of truth or an argument that rests on majority vote. Many will continue to disagree with claims made by Catholics on secular warrant. The point is that if all or most non-Catholics disagree with a Catholic claim on secular warrant, Catholic assumptions about its general availability to persons of intelligence and good will must become suspect, even to Catholics. I take it that this was the purport of Murray's persistent appeal to "the public consensus" as a code word for determining in concrete historical circumstances what Catholics traditionally referred to as natural law.

The third shift is a new Catholic insistence upon seeing natural law as a dynamic process, a reality capable of evolution, advance and regress, moderation, and dramatic restatement under the impact of new historical circumstances. A new and strong sense of historical consciousness no longer allows the social structure of the medieval period to function for Catholics as an ahistorical ideal.

Elements of the Catholic argument for disestablishment, religious liberty, and subsidiarity crosscut other theological and secular positions. The Catholic understandings of the nature and mission of the church are very close to those Protestant positions Sanders calls transformationist. In general, Calvinist theories of church and state will be closer than other Protestant options to Thomistic Catholic positions. In particular, I find John C. Bennett and John Courtney Murray in agreement on almost every substantive ethical and theological warrant for church-state relations.[18]

As regards governmental competence in religion, Catholics may be closest to the strict separationists. The early Baptist Thomas Helwys stated, "For men's religion to God is betwixt God and themselves; the king shall not answer for it, neither may the king judge between God and man.

---

[18] See Gustafson's remarks about family resemblances between Calvinism and Thomism. Ibid., p. 119.

Let them be heretikes, Turcks, Jewes, or whatsoever, it apperteynes not to the earthly power to punish them in the least measure."[19] Although Helwys asserts an individualist notion of religion mostly foreign to Catholics— what Baptists call "soul competency"—he concludes in terms that parallel Murray's assertions, on other grounds, of governmental incompetence to abjudicate in religious matters.

The genius of Murray's theological argument, it seems to me, lies in his ability to appeal simultaneously to a theological source and to correlative secular warrant. Particularist theological symbols firmly anchor Christian or Jewish policy statements on human rights, religious liberty, and the state in the particularist identity of the respective traditions. They serve to motivate believers in their political orientations and public moral stances. They affirm the ways in which faith has public policy implications. In this way believers are moved to engage in what Martin Marty calls public theology. They must articulate the public policy implications of their particularist symbols. On the other hand, the secular warrant has a validity independent of its connection with a particularist Catholic, Protestant, or Jewish theological symbol. The secular warrant opens up possibilities of dialogue with others who do not share the faith vision connected with it. Thus, public theology becomes truly public when it becomes also civil discourse.[20]

A Theological Understanding of the First Amendment

Just as there are two distinct First Amendment provisions on religion— the no-establishment and free exercise clauses—so the Catholic case for the two provisions rests on two very different kinds of arguments, those for disestablishment and those for religious liberty.

Disestablishment. Murray contended that no theological brief could be mounted either to vindicate or to reject the no-establishment clause. That part of the First Amendment had proved useful to the American people,

---

[19] Cited in Sanders, *Protestant Concepts,* p. 172. In a very illuminating remark Sanders claims that the strict separationist theological position, based as it is on individualism (soul competency) and a contract view of the origin of the state, does not do justice to mediating structures. "One finds little or no recognition [in contemporary separationist thought] of the significant pluralistic social philosophy by which the rights of corporate groups are guaranteed and which many interpreters regard as one of the chief characteristics of Anglo-Saxon democracy" (p. 202).

[20] I do not want to enter here into the discussion of how much the civil discourse ideal is ultimately of peculiarly Protestant provenance or the further question of how this civil discourse can emasculate, tame, and denude theological identity. See John Murray Cuddihy, *No Offense: Civil Religion and Protestant Taste* (New York: Seabury Press, 1978).

the state, and the churches. It serves as the first of American prejudices as, in another context, Edmund Burke insisted that establishment was the first of English prejudices.

In the American case, the no-establishment clause is best seen as an article of peace rather than an article of faith. The First Amendment does not assert or imply a particular sectarian or secularist concept of the church or say anything about the ontological nature of truth and freedom or the manner in which the spiritual order of man's life is to be organized or not organized. For if any particular sectarian theses enter into the content or implications of the First Amendment, "the very article that bars any establishment would somehow establish one."[21]

American Catholics in unbroken succession since the beginning of the Republic have insisted—almost in dreary monotony—on their support of the First Amendment because they stand in what Winthrop Hudson calls "the great tradition of the American churches."[22] As Hudson argues, the voluntary church in America has given birth to numerous voluntary societies active in the public interest. These, in turn, spawned secular voluntaryism. The church best flourishes as a free church in an environment where such voluntaryism is strong. As Tocqueville noted, such voluntaryism in the public sector of the national life early set a characteristic stamp of vitality, creativity, and pluralism on American public affairs. The church is strongest both as a church and as a mediating structure in a climate where other, nonchurch mediating structures also thrive. Public recognition and the power of church voluntaryism stand and fall with them. A comparison of American churches with churches struggling to assert their freedom in Brazil, Malawi, or South Korea substantiates this point.

Moreover, as my colleague, Brian Smith, argues, it is precisely those churches with a strong infrastructure of church-sponsored mediating organizations that possess the greatest capability to withstand state tyranny by asserting the claims of religious liberty.[23] They contain the space for free discussion and corporate planning. They also generate motivation in a large clientele. A comparison of the church-state relation in Poland with that in Czechoslovakia and Cuba and of Uruguay with Chile and Brazil validates this contention. As I will show further on, there is both a logical and an empirical link in the argument for religious liberty and the case for

---

[21] Murray, *We Hold These Truths,* p. 63.

[22] Winthrop Hudson, *The Great Tradition of the American Churches* (New York: Harper & Row, 1953).

[23] Brian Smith, "Pastoral Strategy in the Third World," *America,* May 18, 1974, pp. 389–392, and "The Chilean Church and Political Change: 1925–1975," Ph.D. dissertation, Department of Political Science, Yale University, 1979.

mediating structures. Based on the felicitous connection between church voluntaryism and the hitherto voluntary character of American society, which has been the fruit of the no-establishment clause, disestablishment deserves to be the first of our American prejudices.

With a tutored sense for historical and constitutional variation, however, Murray could discover no theological warrant to oppose the notion of establishment in other countries or historical contexts. So long as there is no confusion of the religious and the political, no infringement of the freedom of the church or of the expression of personal conscience, and no alienation of the people from the church through the relation of church and state, a case for establishment might, in principle, be made. The clincher for Murray's contention is his assertion that it is nonsense to speak of an ahistorical constitutional ideal. Murray preferred Plato's *Politics* to *The Laws*. The litmus test for constitutions and juridical systems is their usefulness, their suitability to the mores, history, and peculiar circumstances of a people.

No kind of establishment makes any sense in the American circumstance. Elsewhere, an establishment such as in England or Sweden or a "multiple establishment," which, it is sometimes alleged, characterizes the Netherlands, might be defensible.[24] Under no circumstances, Murray states, can "an argument be made today that would validate the legal institution of religious intolerance."[25]

Murray never contended that U.S. disestablishment should serve as the constitutional ideal of other countries. The concept of one international constitutional ideal is a contradiction in terms. But if the United States is not a constitutional ideal for Catholics, neither is Colombia nor Franco's Spain. As John Murray Cuddihy stated in dealing with the issues of the First Amendment, "Civil religion was knocking at the door. Murray

---

[24] For the nature of Dutch subsidy politics, see Arend Lijphart, *The Politics of Accommodation* (Berkeley: University of California Press, 1968), and John A. Coleman, S.J., *The Evolution of Dutch Catholicism* (Berkeley: University of California Press, 1978), pp. 58–87. The Dutch constitution has stipulated a separation of church and state since 1814. There is no provision that members of the royal family must belong to any religion. It should be noted that secular groups or "ideological families," even though nonreligious, are entitled to state welfare subsidies on exactly the same basis as church groups. A Dutch socialist, secular liberal and member of other nonsectarian groups does not find himself, as Dean Kelley mistakenly suggests, in a position where he has to "go through an alien religious portal to gain his civic benefits." Classical Dutch *Verzuiling,* as I argue in my book, contained many problems as a way of dealing with pluralism. Neither religious establishment nor the violation of religious liberty seem to me to be among those problems. The Dutch government does not pay the salary of ministers or for the upkeep of churches, unless they are declared historical monuments.

[25] Murray, *Problem of Religious Freedom,* p. 203.

refused to open it."[26] Instead, Murray opted for the conditions of civility, an interpretation of the no-establishment clause as an article of peace. The First Amendment clauses are a statement of policy. They are not deontological principles representing moral absolutes, nor are they self-interpreting. Various interpretations of them clash in law. None is established as doctrine. Catholics give to these articles of law absolutely no religious assent. They obey, support, and uphold them on moral grounds, because they are good law. Catholic "commitment is limited in the sense that it is not to the truth and sanctity of a dogma but only to the rationality and goodness of a law." For Murray, "this is all that need be shown; it is likewise all that can be shown."[27]

The Constitution, Murray insisted, is not a theological but a political document, defining the concept of the state, not of a church.[28] The concept of the state defined by the no-establishment clause is that of a limited constitutional state that acknowledges its own incompetency to judge in areas spiritual or religious. The clause is simply silent about the competencies of the church. The state's proper domain is the temporal common good, the arena of peace, public order, the public welfare, distributive justice, and the protection and enhancement of the people's freedoms.

The only circumstances in which the state, as a guardian of the temporal common good, might act to restrict claims to public religious expressions are when such expressions represent serious, clear, and present dangers to public order and peace. Murray was stringent in placing conditions on any state intervention in religious matters touching the public order: the violation must be really serious; state intervention must be really necessary and a last resort; regard must be had for the privileged character of religious freedom; and the rule of jurisprudence of a free society must be strictly followed.[29] As an article of peace the First Amendment permits state intervention in areas touching religion only when the public peace urgently commands it. The presumption always lies against such intervention until sufficient proof warrants the contrary. For, in Elizabeth I's exquisite phrase, "No government may make windows to men's souls." As Murray put it, "The public powers are not competent to make theological judgments. . . . The public powers are not competent to inquire into the norms whereby conscience is formed and to judge their truth or falsity."[30]

---

[26] Cuddihy, *No Offense,* p. 72.

[27] Murray, *We Hold These Truths,* p. 85.

[28] Cuddihy, *No Offense,* p. 74.

[29] Murray, *Problem of Religious Freedom,* p. 45.

[30] Ibid., p. 42.

A major element in Murray's historical reconstruction of Catholic church-state doctrine depended on his historical judgment that the U.S. disestablishment differed radically from the European secularist or laicist state condemned by the popes, where religious authority depended on the good graces of the state. In France, Germany, Mexico, and elsewhere serious efforts were undertaken to restrict religious activity to the sanctuary and the sacristy. Significantly, the church's ability to generate its own mediating structures—schools, hospitals, charity organizations—was severely curtailed. In the United States, Murray claimed, "It is contrary to the American tradition to view separation of church and state as a categorical absolute, to be rigidly enforced, no matter what may be the effects on free exercise of religion. . . [for] the whole intent of the First Amendment was to protect, not to injure, the interests of religion in American society."[31] The two clauses of the First Amendment exist in dialectical tension. They comment on each other.

Murray could feel secure in his interpretation of the First Amendment because it is widely shared by non-Catholics. Thus, John Bennett contends that "our nation or state is not in principle secular or even neutral as between religion and the rejection of it."[32] In his characteristic wisdom, Bennett goes on to assert, "We have to weigh the negative religious freedom of a small minority over against the positive religious freedom of the vast majority. In doing so, we should protest this negative religious freedom to the extent that it involves freedom to express opposition to religion. We should not, in protecting it, deny to most people opportunities for positive religious expression in the context of their national life."[33] The Quaker, Wilmer Cooper, concurs:

> It was certainly not the intention of our founding fathers, who made provisions for the separation of church and state in our constitution, to divorce religion from politics. What they were concerned about was that there be no particular establishment of religion or preferential treatment of one religion as opposed to another, but this is not to say that religion should have no influence upon government and political decisions.[34]

Finally, the Supreme Court itself had declared, "The First Amendment . . . does not say that in every and all respects there shall be a separation of church and state. . . . Otherwise, the state and religion would be aliens to

---

[31] Murray, *We Hold These Truths,* p. 150.
[32] Bennett, *Christians and the State,* p. 5.
[33] Ibid., p. 10.
[34] Cited in Sanders, *Protestant Concepts,* p. 145.

each other—hostile, suspicious, and even unfriendly. . . . We are a religious people, whose institutions presuppose a Supreme Being."[35]

The unrestricted moral consent of American Catholics to the First Amendment flows from this kind of interpretation. America differed from the laicist France of the Third Republic precisely because, as John Bennett states, "The American system of church-state separation was not the result of hostility to Christianity or of the desire to put the churches at a disadvantage."[36] Indeed, the First Amendment, in this view, represents the classic example of governmental care for religion by its scrupulous care for the freedom of religion, which is precisely what Catholic theology demands of the state. As explained in *Dignitatis Humanae,*

> In turn, where the principle of religious freedom is not only proclaimed in words or simply incorporated in law but also given sincere and practical application, there the church succeeds in achieving a stable situation of right as well as of fact and the independence which is necessary for the fulfillment of her divine mission. This independence is precisely what the authorities of the church claim in society.[37]

Because the Catholic case for American disestablishment is moral rather than religious, an adherence to good law instead of to religious dogma, American Catholics contend that they enjoy the right, no less than others, to press for the legal resolution of disputed interpretations of the First Amendment. They do not feel bound to obey, in advance, interpretations of the First Amendment that are not yet law. Their case for religious freedom rests on religious as well as on legal norms.

Thus, Catholics champion the so-called Kurland rule, which states that it is not unconstitutional for a law having proper secular objectives incidentally to benefit religion. Catholics support the rule because it strikes them as sane public policy and protects their claim on theological grounds for the effective freedom of the church. Of course, the rule is also in their self-interest. Unless something like the Kurland rule obtains, the First Amendment becomes a serious penalty for religion by placing religious activity in an unfair competitive position vis-à-vis secularism. For the danger of totalitarian democracy lies in a state monopoly in the public sector. Or, if the state subsidizes only nonreligious voluntary organizations, it is exercising a preferential establishment of a religious position.

In effect, the social situation that relegates religious activity more and more to the sanctuary could be acceptable only to those who follow

---

[35] Zorach v. Clauson, 343 U.S. 306 (1952).

[36] Bennett, *Christians and the State,* p. 209.

[37] O'Brien and Shannon, *Renewing the Earth,* p. 302.

35

Dean Kelley in drawing sharp distinctions between religious meaning and social service, education, and public activity. For many religious believers, this distinction betrays the very caritative mission of the church, its call to combat and to transform sinful social structures as part of its obedient hearing of the word of God. For many, the effective absence of religious voice from key areas of the public sector is a kind of false statement about the role and function of religion in society. It is important to note that many of Kelley's policy proposals depend on his particular view of the church, his ecclesiology, rather than on secular warrant. The danger of further privatization of religion by restricting its activity to the sanctuary and its own parochial grounds led James Rausch to observe, "What must be constantly watched is any attempt in the practical or theoretical order, coming from within the church or without, to translate the separation of church and state into a prevailing doctrine of separating the church from society."[38]

The public Catholic case for the Kurland interpretation of the First Amendment, touching a disputed issue in law, rests entirely on secular warrant. No one is asked to ascribe to the Catholic self-understanding of the mission of the church or the particularist grounds for asserting the fact and scope of the freedom of the church. Civil as opposed to theological discourse appeals to norms of distributive justice, the public good, the value of pluralism for the social order, and the wisdom of structuring society in ways that encourage, promote, and utilize mediating structures. While the theological case depends on civil warrants as an integral part of the structure of its argument, in no sense does the civil warrant necessarily rest on any appeal to particularist theological creed.

In a similar way, Catholic pleas that the state recognize the double financial burden of parents who send their children to private or parochial schools rely on the norm of distributive justice in adjudicating burdens and benefits within society. They also ask for effective state recognition of the fundamental right of parents to determine the style of education for their children. At present, this parental right represents a special burden which penalizes parents who choose to exercise it. Catholics also claim that the state should acknowledge the public services rendered to society by parochial and private schools. Finally, they cite the societal good derived from competition and pluralism in alternative school systems. Catholics do not claim they have any religious right to federal or state aid. Nor do they ask for a special privilege that would be withheld from other parents—Jews, Episcopalians, Seventh-Day Adventists, Missouri Synod Lutherans, secularists—suffering double taxation.

---

[38] Rausch, "Dignitatis Humanae," p. 43.

I know of very few Catholics who are not persuaded of the justice of state aid to parents or students in parochial and private schools. They argue that in areas such as education and welfare where the state rightly claims an interest, the state should also allow some choice and pluralism. I know of even fewer Catholics who can divine any cogent differences between permissible aid to sectarian colleges and universities and non-permissible aid to primary and secondary schools. The interests lobbying for the former, of course, include powerful private universities with political influence. To Catholics the arguments for aid in the two cases seem roughly parallel.

Some Catholics argue that it is preferable to forgo their rights to relief from double education costs either in the interest of ecumenical peace or, following Dean Kelley, to forestall the situation by which "the 'Queen's shilling' will sooner or later be followed by the Queen." I will not enter here into discussion of the numerous ways it is possible to build protections into public policy against the Queen following the Queen's shilling when it is in the public interest to separate financial subsidy from outright control. The government-sponsored British Broadcasting Company is the classic example of that possibility.

My point here is that choosing to forgo the pressing of a right or to be fatalistic about its being accepted as a right in a pluralistic context is something other than a denial of a just basis for the claim. It might, of course, be possible to make a suasive case that even indirect aid to church-sponsored and private schools would necessarily and seriously undermine support for quality public schools or lead to fragmented and antagonistic subcultures within society. In that case, the argument against aid to parents and students in parochial and private schools should be properly couched in terms of the public good. It is simply wrong to assert that such aid is per se an issue of the First Amendment. For the Catholic case for aid for parents and students in parochial schools is not raised in terms of claims of true religion or of preferential treatment for Catholic or even religious schools. The question is phrased, as Murray raised it, in secular moral terms, "Is it justice?"

Religious Liberty. Liberty of conscience and public freedom of personal and ecclesial religious expression rest on a firmer Catholic theological basis than does disestablishment. The normative conciliar document *Dignitatis Humanae* looks both to the revealed word of God and to reason itself to ground the base point for religious liberty: the dignity of the human person. It is a mistake of category in the use of language to assert that either truth or error has any rights. If a right is defined as an urgent moral claim on another to respect an immunity or to deliver a good that is in the other's power to grant, it may even be a mistake of language to

37

assert rights of God. He is beyond the realm of claims. Only persons enjoy rights.

Dignitatis Humanae asserts that every person enjoys the right to religious liberty because, in Catholic theology, the act of faith, to be truly human, must eventuate from a free response to the initiative of God. A second theological argument for religious liberty insists that the authority of the church in no way derives from the state but flows directly from obedience to God. The authority of the state, however, derives indirectly from God through the people, in whom sovereign authority ultimately rests. The state exists to serve the needs and interests of the people. Its authority is instrumental, not substantive. Murray, citing the Gelasian maxim, refers to these two kinds of authority as a dyarchy: "Two there are, August Emperor, by which this world is ruled on title of original and sovereign right—the consecrated authority of the priesthood and the royal power." Hence, he further asserts, "By divine authority this world is to be ruled by a dyarchy of authorities, within which the temporal is subordinate to the spiritual, not instrumentally but in dignity."[39] The sign of that subordination is the state's recognition of its incompetency in matters religious. As stated in *Dignitatis Humanae,* it follows from this sense of dyarchy that "the freedom of the church is the fundamental principle in what concerns the relations between the church and governments and the whole civil order."[40] As James Rausch puts it, "The church . . . seeks neither privilege nor special protection from the state, only the freedom to fulfill its religious mission and ministry to society."[41]

Dignitatis Humanae also structures a moral argument for religious liberty. It appeals to human dignity, the *res sacra homo.* Every person "has the right and duty to seek the truth in matters religious."[42] Persons are endowed with dignity by reason of their freedom and intelligence. They are privileged to bear responsibility toward the truth and for their own self-chosen identity as moral agents. Each person has an inescapable responsibility to establish his or her unique relationship to God. No other person or agency—family, church, or state—may assume this responsibility nor coerce the individual's choice in such matters.

Human dignity is in no way conditional on personal merit or subjective character. It is ontologically grounded in the very fact of personhood. Thus, *Dignitatis Humanae* asserts that "the right to religious freedom has its foundation, not in the subjective disposition of the person but in his

---

[39] Murray, *We Hold These Truths,* p. 32.

[40] O'Brien and Shannon, *Renewing the Earth,* p. 302.

[41] Rausch, "Dignitatis Humanae," p. 41.

[42] O'Brien and Shannon, *Renewing the Earth,* p. 293.

very nature."[43] This moral argument, based on secular warrant, should find resonance among those who, with Emile Durkheim, see that in modern societies under conditions of religious pluralism only justice and the sacred character of the individual—*res sacra homo*—and his groups can function as the indispensable collective conscience and civil religion.[44]

Religious liberty in the Second Vatican Council document involves a twofold immunity. No one "is to be forced to act in a manner contrary to his conscience. Nor, on the other hand, is he to be restrained from acting in accordance with his conscience, especially in matters religious."[45] The second immunity was denied in preconciliar Catholic teaching, at least in regard to the public expression of religion, because of a traditional Catholic insistence that societies, as well as individuals, have obligations toward God and truth. This insistence is the characteristic Catholic way of holding to the indispensable concept of the sovereignty of God over society and nations and of fending off excessive individualism and the privatization of religion. It is a matter of Catholic belief that every nation exists under the judgment of God.

This more traditional Catholic understanding that denied freedom to the public expression of non-Catholic religions was undercut by two crucial distinctions in *Dignitatis Humanae*. The first is the acknowledgment of a necessary connection between private belief and public expression. The connecting link is the social nature of man.

> The social nature of man itself requires that he should give external expression to his internal acts of religion, that he should participate with others in matters religious, that he should profess his religion in community. Injury, therefore, is done to the human person and to the very order established by God for human life, if the free exercise of religion is denied in society when the requirements of public order do not so require.[46]

The second distinction, essential to the shift away from the traditional prohibition of the public expression of non-Catholic religion, is between society and the state. Development of this distinction bears out my contention that the Catholic argument for religious liberty is simultaneously a

---

[43] Ibid.

[44] Emile Durkheim, "Individualism and the Intellectuals," in Robert N. Bellah, ed., *Emile Durkheim on Morality and Society* (Chicago: University of Chicago Press, 1973), pp. 43–58.

[45] O'Brien and Shannon, *Renewing the Earth*, p. 293.

[46] Ibid., p. 294.

strong case for mediating structures. The text that needs explaining, at least to non-Catholics, reads in *Dignitatis Humanae:*

> The truth can not impose itself except by virtue of its own truth, as it makes its entrance into the mind at once quietly and with power. Religious freedom, in turn, which men deemed as necessary to fulfill their duty to worship God has to do with immunity from coercion in civil society. Therefore, *it leaves untouched the moral duty of men and societies toward the true religion. . . .*[47]

The italicized lines indicate that Catholics have not abandoned their belief that God is sovereign over society and that it is incumbent upon society to recognize its dependence on God. One indication of this sovereignty is the state's recognition of the church's claim for juridical immunity in religious matters. By appealing to the distinction between society and the state, Murray shifted the burden of public acknowledgment of the sovereignty of God from the state—which is, in any event, incompetent in religious matters—to the wider society, the people acting through their voluntary mediating structures and corporate groups. The freedom asserted in *Dignitatis Humanae* as a limit on state power is more than the freedom of the church or of individual religious conscience. The document signals as well the rightful freedom of mediating corporate groups. Indeed, it envisions as normative neither the confessional state nor the laicist secular state but the limited constitutional state. There is a juridical as well as a moral and theological promise to *Dignitatis Humanae:* "The demand is also made that constitutional limits should be set to the powers of government in order that there may be no encroachment on the rightful freedom of the person *and of associations.*"[48]

The state's care for true religion is restricted to its care for the freedom of religion. Society's obligation to care for religion is more extensive. The fulfillment of society's religious duty depends on an interpretation of the First Amendment that would allow some controlled contact and cooperation between the autonomous state and the several independent churches. The free people, organized through their own mediating structures, not the state as such, express and acknowledge the sovereignty of God over the society and nation. Murray maintains

> in common with all Catholics that an obligation to profess faith in God and to worship him is incumbent on society—on the people as such as well as on individuals; this obligation, however, is not fulfilled by a legislative or executive action by the

---

[47] Ibid., p. 292. Emphasis added.
[48] Ibid., p. 297. Emphasis added.

public power. It is fulfilled by occasional public acts of worship on so-called state occasions. These acts of worship are organized by the church, not the government, which has no competence in liturgical matters. Moreover, they are voluntary acts, since they are formally acts of religion.[49]

While no one should be coerced into religious behavior, neither should others be restrained from a public expression of religion in the context of the national life.

State versus Society

In its distinction between state and society, Catholic social thought contains a strong animus against the view that the public sphere is synonymous with the government or the formal polity of the society. It does not assume that everything public must ipso facto be governmental. In distinguishing between state and society it also distinguishes between the public order entrusted to the state—an order of unity, coercion, and necessity—and the common good, which is entrusted to the whole society, a zone of comparative freedom and pluralism. As the abnormal instance of societies under foreign occupation makes evident, this distinction between state and society makes eminent empirical sense.

Even in the normal case, however, there is a proper distinction between state and society. Catholic social thought is pluralistic in its insistence on the limited, service character of the state. The state exists as an instrument to promote justice and liberty. There are four ends of the public order entrusted uniquely to the state: public peace, public morality, welfare and justice, and the freedom of the people. As Murray explains, "The democratic state serves both the ends of the human person (in itself and its natural forms of social life) and also the ends of justice. As the servant of these ends, it has only relative value."[50] If the state is both subject to and the servant of the common good, it "is not the sole judge of what is or is not the common good." Moreover, "in consequence of the distinction between society and state, not every element of the common good is instantly committed to the state to be protected and promoted." On the contrary, "government submits itself to judgment by the truth of society; it is not itself a judge of the truth in society."[51]

Perhaps the clearest and most developed statement of the distinction between society and the state is found in Maritain's classic book *Man and*

---

[49] Murray, *Problem of Religious Freedom*, p. 93.
[50] Murray, *We Told These Truths*, p. 308.
[51] Murray, *Problem of Religious Freedom*, p. 42.

the State, on which Murray relied. Maritain ascribes to the state an instrumental, service character that is a part—the topmost part and agency—of the whole society, which he calls "the body politic." The state is the part that specializes in the interest of the whole. Its authority is derivative. It exists not by its own right and for its own sake but only in virtue and to the extent of the requirements of the common good. At least two corporate units in society, the family and the church, have rights and freedoms anterior to the state. Other corporate units—voluntary associations such as universities, unions, agencies in the public interest—stake out a zone of free sociality in society. The right to voluntary association is based on the social nature of man whose sociality is not exhausted by citizenship in the state. Maritain asserts that "the state is inferior to the body politic as a whole and is at the service of the body politic as a whole."[52] He denies that the state is a moral personality, the subject of rights, or in any sense the head of the body politic. It serves a purely instrumental role in the service of the people, the proper subject of rights.

Maritain argues that mediating structures should be as autonomous as possible because family, economic, cultural, educational, and religious life matter as much as does political life to the very existence and prosperity of the body politic. Normally, the principle of subsidiarity should govern the relation between the state and mediating structures "since in political society authority comes from below through the people. It is normal that the whole dynamism of authority in the body politic should be made up of particular and partial authorities rising in tiers above one another up to the top authority of the state."[53]

Subsidiarity is an esoteric Catholic term, first coined in 1931 by Pius XI in his encyclical, *Quadragesimo Anno,* although the principle to which it points has long existed in democratic pluralist theory. It is a derivative rule of the state-society distinction to delineate both the moral right and the moral limitations of state intervention in cultural, social, and economic affairs. Its formulation reads:

> It is a fundamental principle of social philosophy . . . that one should not withdraw from individuals and commit to the community what they can accomplish by their own enterprise and industry. So, too, it is an injustice and at the same time a grave evil and a disturbance of right order, to transfer to the larger and higher collectivity functions which can be performed and provided by the lesser and subordinate bodies. Inasmuch as

---

[52] Maritain, *Man and the State,* p. 13.
[53] Ibid., p. 11.

every social activity should, by its very nature, prove a help to members of the body social, it should never destroy or absorb them.[54]

While the term is esoteric, because Catholic, the concept is not. Subsidiarity is in no sense a religious concept. It rests entirely on secular warrant. It grew out of reflection on social experience, not revelation. Catholic social thought looks to it as a congealment of historic wisdom about the arrangement of social orders. It is a presumptive rule about where real vitality exists in society. Clearly, as *Quadragesimo Anno* realized and John XXIII's *Mater et Magistra* (1961) made very clear, the state can and must intervene for public welfare when intermediate associations are deficient. But the presumption is that such intervention, while justified, should never "destroy or absorb" the lesser or subordinate bodies. The principle of subsidiarity is simply a version of the theory of democratic pluralism to be found, in more secular guise, in Tocqueville, Durkheim, and, more recently, E. F. Schumacher and Michael Walzer.[55]

The case for subsidiarity can be made on different theological and social grounds. Thus, Anabaptists argue that "the real dynamic of society does not lie in the state; state action is obviated when subordinate groups, like the church, effectively deal with education, health, relief and social security. Christians should not rely too much on the state and thus become completely obligated to it."[56] Some Protestant thinkers appeal to the concept—not the term—in their insistence on the sinful corruption of power and the need for countervailing power to check the all-powerful state. One Dutch Calvinist group, the *Gereformeerden,* has concluded to something like it in their translation of the sovereignty of God to mean "sovereignty in our own circle." *Gereformeerden* church control over their own mediating structures serves as a crucial check on idolatrous claims of state sovereignty, even when the state provides subsidy. The Netherlands is, perhaps, the paradise for mediating structures and the principle of subsidiarity, and it is clear to anyone who knows Dutch history that a Calvinist, Abraham Kuyper, was the principal architect of the Dutch subsidiarity state.

The secular warrants for subsidiarity are many. Thus, E. F. Schumacher contends that the principle is a rule for efficiency, the best way to

---

[54] Cited in O'Brien and Shannon, *Renewing the Earth,* p. 62.

[55] See Michael Walzer, "The Problem of Citizenship," in *Obligations: Essays on Disobedience, War and Citizenship* (Cambridge: Harvard University Press, 1970), pp. 203–228.

[56] Cited in Sanders, *Protestant Concepts,* p. 107.

increase both productivity and participant satisfaction. Berger and Neu-haus argue that a society governed by subsidiarity is more humane since "human beings understand their own needs better than anyone else—in, say, 99 percent of all cases."[57] H. A. Rommen insists on intermediate structures as a fountain of creativity and experiment: "The state is not creative but individual persons in their free association and their group life are creative."[58]

Maritain's argument for subsidiarity is redolent of Emile Durkheim's communication theory of government in *Professional Morals and Civic Ethics,* where Durkheim pleads for intermediate associations because the state is too abstract and distant.[59] As Maritain argues, "To become a boss or a manager in business or industry or a patron of art or a leading spirit in the affairs of culture, science and philosophy is against the nature of such an impersonal topmost agency, abstract so to speak, and separated from the moving peculiarities, mutual tensions, risks, and dynamism of concrete social existence."[60] Andrew Greeley appeals to subsidiarity as a bulwark for freedom:

> The principle of subsidiarity—no bigger than necessary—is fundamental precisely because it is a guarantee of personal freedom. . . . Freedom is ultimately facilitated by having roots, by having a place to call home, by having a group to which one belongs. . . . You can't be free without belonging, you can't be autonomous without being committed, you can't be independ-ent without being secure, you can't go somewhere else unless you can go home again.[61]

Nor are Catholics the only religious body to espouse this wisdom. The World Council of Churches asserted in its Evanston Assembly (1954) that "forms of association within society which have their own foundation and principles should be respected and not controlled in their inner life by the state. Churches, families and universities are dissimilar examples of this nonpolitical type of association."[62]

The principle of subsidiarity is not writ large on the fabric of the universe because it is distilled wisdom, an empirical generalization and a maxim for ordering a sane society rather than an ontological principle or

---

[57] Peter L. Berger and Richard John Neuhaus, *To Empower People: The Role of Mediating Structures in Public Policy* (Washington, D.C.: American Enterprise In-stitute, 1977), p. 7.

[58] Rommen, *State of Catholic Thought,* p. 253.

[59] Emile Durkheim, *Professional Morals and Civic Ethics* (London: Routledge and Kegan Paul, 1957), p. 73 ff.

[60] Maritain, *Man and the State,* p. 21.

[61] Andrew Greeley, *Neighborhood* (New York: Seabury Press, 1977), p. 68.

[62] Cited in Bennett, *Christians and the State,* p. 77.

a phenomenological description of how states always or actually operate. The principle is of renewed interest today precisely because of two new threats to the voluntary society. The first is the extensive growth of welfare organized by the state, which will not be dismantled for romantic visions of a simpler agrarian society. The modern state, by reason of its duty to enforce and promote social justice, has inevitably and properly moved into a vacuum to make up for deficiencies of a society whose basic mediating structures cannot provide universal welfare and justice. The second danger stems from the fact that increased governmental intervention in the name of welfare is coupled with what Ivan Illich refers to as "professional monopoly." Detailed regulations, certification, and preconditions imposed upon the service sector of society are pricing voluntary agencies out of the market. The voluntary society is in a new danger and with it, human freedom, humane scale, and local corporate wisdom and creativity.

Berger and Neuhaus's three policy propositions on mediating structures are a fair capsule of the biases of Catholic social theory and the principle of subsidiarity: (1) mediating structures are essential for a vital democratic society; (2) public policy should protect and foster mediating structures; and (3) wherever possible, public policy should utilize mediating structures for the realization of social purposes.[63] Maritain makes a similar claim: "Civil legislation should adapt itself to the variety of moral creeds of the diverse spiritual lineages which essentially bear on the common good of the social body—not by endorsing them or approving them but rather by giving allowance to them."[64]

The principle of subsidiarity is a subset rule of the larger distinction between state and society. The sign that this distinction is not just an abstraction is the presence of multiple, vigorous, voluntary associations acting in the public sphere and cooperating and competing with the government in defining the common good. It is simply not true, as Kelley asserts in his essay, that the lower authority envisioned by the principle of subsidiarity is exclusively or primarily the church or local communities served by the church. The literature on subsidiarity cites primarily universities, trade and credit unions, cooperatives, neighborhoods, and regional associations. Indeed, in neither *Quadragesimo Anno* nor *Mater et Magistra* is the principle even directly applied to the church, although such application is not excluded. The church and its agencies (the latter often only tenuously connected to the church juridically when they represent what Maritain refers to as associations of Christian inspiration as opposed to units of the church) seek neither preferential treatment nor protection.

---

[63] Berger and Neuhaus, *To Empower People*, p. 6.
[64] Maritain, *Man and the State*, p. 169.

45

They merely desire that they not be excluded from protections and benefits granted to all intermediate associations, secular or religious. They can argue that such exclusion is tantamount to the denial to them of freedom of religious expression.

It is also not true that the principle of subsidiarity asserts that the government should subsidize without monitoring how its money is spent. As the principle is stated in *Mater et Magistra,* both the competency of government (it "encourages, stimulates, regulates, supplements and complements") and its limitations (it does not destroy or absorb mediating structures) are clearly set forth.[65]

The key link between the Catholic case for religious liberty and the case for subsidiarity is dependent on an understanding of religious activity and expression as something more than "providing meaning in the sanctuary." As *Dignitatis Humanae* states:

> In addition, it comes within the meaning of religious freedom that religious bodies should not be prohibited from freely undertaking to show the special value of their doctrine in what concerns the organization of society and the inspiration of the whole of human activity. Finally, the social nature of man and the very nature of religion afford the foundation of the right of men freely to hold meetings and to establish educational, cultural, charitable and social organizations, under the impulse of their own religious sense.[66]

The connection between church-state theory and church-society relations is clear. The First Amendment must not impede or penalize the freedom of the church to pursue its mission in society as it understands it. But the church's self-understanding in terms of its mission to society rests on particularist theological warrant. We cannot expect that self-understanding to become public property enshrined in law. The church can garner public support for the freedom it demands for itself in fidelity to gospel warrant only if it states its case simultaneously on secular warrant. The secular warrant is the argument for mediating structures as a key element in public policy. For, as Murray clearly saw, the freedom of the church is linked inextricably to other civil freedoms: "The personal and corporate free exercise of religion as a human and civil right is evidently cognate with other more general human and civil rights—with the freedom of corporate bodies and institutions within society, based on the principle of subsidiary functions; with the general freedom of speech and of the press based on the nature of political society."[67]

---

[65] O'Brien and Shannon, *Renewing the Earth,* pp. 62–63.

[66] Ibid., p. 295.

[67] Murray, *Problems of Religious Freedom,* pp. 26–27.

The long lessons of history and the recent struggles of the church in Latin America and East Africa make clear that the voluntary church only flourishes in climates where voluntaryism is generally prized in the wider society. Churches that understand their mission in society beyond the narrow confines of the sanctuary depend upon an interpretation of church-state separation that encourages intermediate associations generally. The secular warrant that mediates the church's theological understanding of its mission to society as part of its essential role is a social philosophy that insists on the distinction between society and the state and the concomitant obligation of the state to protect, nurture, and promote mediating structures as vital to the society. Catholics will grant a theological balance to mediating structures beyond their secular warrant since a climate that nourishes them is essential to the freedom and scope of religious activity called for by *Gaudium et Spes* and the Bishops' Synod document on *Justice in the World.*

I agree with Kelley that churches are not just mediating structures. They have other functions, especially that of providing meaning, identity, belonging, and commitment to transcendent truth. I do not, however, on theological grounds, think that these other functions are intrinsically more important or that mediation is necessarily a distraction for the church. As I understand the thrust of postconciliar Catholic theology, the church exists precisely for mission and ministry to the world. Service to the world is not something the church does after being fully constituted. It is not a luxury. The church's very ingathering, its nature as community, is constituted by its being sent in mission. Its mission, moreover, depends on its ability to function as a mediating structure. Therefore, its freedom to be itself is threatened whenever the general climate for mediating structures is endangered. In championing the rights of other nonreligious mediating structures in society the church is protecting its own interests and its own freedom. For, as Murray saw, when insisting on a juridical component in the final version of *Dignitatis Humanae,* a claim in society under the rubric of civil discourse for freedom for the church is simultaneously a plea for similar liberty for other intermediate associations: "Constitutional government, limited in its powers, dedicated to the defense of the rights of man and to the promotion of the freedom of the people, is the correlate of religious freedom as a juridical notion, a civil and human right, personal and corporate."[68] In this sense he could state that "in the present moment of history the freedom of the people of God is inseparably linked to the freedom of the people."[69]

I do not expect any non-Catholics to agree with my theology of the

---

[68] Ibid., p. 67.
[69] Ibid., p. 70.

church and its mission to society. Neither do I assume that they will necessarily concur with the Catholic way of construing a theology of church and state. I have rehearsed it here as an exercise in public theology to show the public policy implications of a particular theological position. It may be of interest to others, as it was to me, to discover that the Catholic case for religious liberty depends both on the distinction between state and society and on the principle of subsidiarity as middle terms in an argument supporting, on theological grounds, public religious liberty of non-Catholic churches. The only way to make the Catholic case for religious liberty in civil discourse and on secular warrant is by making a simultaneous case for the freedom and vigor of other, nonreligious, mediating structures. The Catholic understanding of the mission of the church will be diminished or frustrated in societies that construe separation of church and state so narrowly that voluntaryism as a vigorous aspect of public life begins to wane.

But apart from the particularist Catholic theological case for the freedom of the church and religious liberty, there are sufficient secular warrants to consider the wisdom and usefulness of subsidiarity and mediating structures as public policies on their own merits. As an exercise in civil discourse I propose that we do so. The obstacle to this discourse will be narrow notions of the intent of separation of church and state, which might sacrifice voluntaryism to shore up some imagined wall. I suggest that we listen again to the plea Jacques Maritain made to Americans in *Man and the State* concerning the interpretation of the First Amendment: "Sharp distinction *and* actual cooperation, that is an historical treasure the value of which a European is perhaps more prepared to appreciate because of his own bitter experiences. Please to God that you keep it carefully, and do not let your concept of separation veer round to the European one."[70]

---

[70] Maritain, *Man and the State*, p. 183.

Mediating Structures and Constitutional Liberty: Some Current Situations

William Bentley Ball

A subtitle to these remarks should doubtless be *"To Empower People: A Tribute."* That immensely worthwhile essay is a revelation in the most pleasing sense: it says what we at once recognize to be right, and what we had been groping toward, without having had the point in full focus.

There are those of us whose job seems always to be immediate problem solving. We feel like people frantically piling up rocks in the hope that we are building something. Richard Neuhaus and Peter Berger tap us on the shoulder in the midst of our desperate labors and show us a superb portrait. With surprise, we then see resemblances between our haphazard rock pile and the city of good "mediating structures" which the authors have portrayed. And that, indeed, affords hope.

As a lawyer, I have approached this conference with the question: Do we need mediating structures in a society governed by the American Constitution? If the function of the Constitution is to protect the individual from the state, why are mediating structures necessary? Neuhaus and Berger, of course, suggest that the Constitution does not always suffice; indeed, they say that its protections, in some instances, have the effect of enforcing the anarchic will of the individual at the expense of the community. Jacques Maritain notes that strains of eighteenth century rationalism, still active in our constitutional life, promote such results. At the same time, he notes, forms of nineteenth century liberalism have produced an opposite tendency—statism.[1] So today we see two forces moving across the social fabric of America—anarchic individualism and growing state social monopoly. Both, of course, militate against the values which *To Empower People* promotes.

At the present time, mediating structures are not advancing and proliferating. On the contrary, a war to obliterate them is taking place, and there is not even a beleaguered battle line at which their defenders attempt a stand. There are almost no defenders of mediating structures.

Mr. Ball is a partner in the law firm of Ball & Skelly, Harrisburg, Pennsylvania.

[1] Jacques Maritain, *Man and the State* (Chicago: University of Chicago Press, 1951), p. 18.

Private schools, hospitals, and child-caring institutions are being abandoned. Why are those who should be mounting a counteroffensive taking to their heels instead? And why is the attack on mediating structures so intense?

The answer, I believe, is found in the fact that government in America has become an industry—greater, more dynamic, wealthier, and more expansionist than the capitalism of the Harrimans and Rockefellers ever was in its nineteenth century heyday. Government is the direct source of livelihood for a substantial percentage of our population. Further, there is an increasingly pervasive view in government that individuality, to the extent that it is allowable, may exist only in ways the government prescribes. Government agents are trained to recite respect for pluralism in health care or education, for example, just as long as the particular manifestation of pluralism is not an initiative-taking place *outside* governmental purview.

In the health care area, under new federal law, local health agencies are neither mandated nor empowered to take into consideration the religious character of a particular hospital or the religious needs of the community they serve. While proponents of the legislation said many nice things about "the distinctive contributions of the voluntary sector," one of the chief contributions of that sector was ignored (namely, its capacity to respond to the needs of particular groups of individuals and thus act as a mediating structure).

In the education field, recent attempts of government to promote monopoly by talking pluralism represents new heights of progress in doubletalk. Take, for example, this passage from Kentucky's "Standards for Accrediting Elementary Schools" (which that state seeks to apply to all private schools). Standard II is entitled "Statement of Philosophy and Objectives." It says, in part:

> Each school shall develop educational beliefs and objectives
> which reflect: (1) the unique needs of all the pupils it serves;
> (2) the values of human traditions; and, (3) the involvement
> of parents/guardians and the community at large.

This paragraph is set in the midst of a comprehensive regulatory program whereby the state defines, to a considerable extent, the education which the private school may offer. Even apart from that, the above standard itself puts private education within state confines. Besides giving the rather odd command that a private school (or any school) develop educational "beliefs," the state tells the school that those beliefs must reflect "the involvement of the community at large." Thus, a Seventh-Day Adventist school located in a large city would apparently be required to conduct a city-wide consultation which that school's beliefs and objectives would then have to reflect. (Should not then a public school located in a 90 percent Polish Catholic neighborhood, or a Hasidic school located in a largely black, Protestant community, be forced to reflect their settings?)

When I speak of the governmental "attack" on mediating structures in the health, educational, and charitable fields, I do not mean to suggest that state authorities manifest a conscious design to single out and penalize or obliterate the structures. Instead, governmental endeavors usually start with a totally innocent assumption of total governmental competency. Hostility usually sets in only when the assumption of superiority is questioned. Government administrators see such questioning, first, as a showing of ignorance and disobedience and, second, as a threat to the industry that is the source of their income, security, perquisites, and social rank.

Of course there are mendacious public servants and movements within government that deliberately push for ideological goals that suppress the freedom for which *To Empower People* speaks. Obviously, it is a mixed picture. We who would save mediating structures and advance them should not necessarily assume evil intentions on the part of government servants who act against them; neither should we assume that such intentions do *not* exist. As someone remarked: "Just because you're not paranoid doesn't mean they aren't out to get you."

Mediating structures, as I see them, "empower" people in precise harmony with the Constitution, and they are protected by the Constitution—or should be. The Constitution's preamble says that "we, the people" have made our Constitution for the sake of a better union, for justice's sake, to have domestic tranquillity, to defend ourselves, to promote our general welfare, and to "secure the blessings of liberty." There are natural groupings in society which also promote those ends, some being so intimately related to the enjoyment of those ends that they are indispensable. It is all very well to say that the First Amendment protects a person's right to worship in the way he pleases, but if we were to say that his right does not extend to worshipping with a group in church, we have obviously denied him one of the prime "blessings of liberty."

"Blessings of liberty," as the preamble says, do not exist merely for individuals, but "for ourselves and our posterity." The courts have long recognized that at least some natural groupings enjoy liberties *as groupings,* apart from the individuals who make them up. The Supreme Court has held that the religious liberty of churches is protected by the Constitution. As recently as 1976, in a case involving the Serbian Orthodox Church, the Court reiterated its century-old insistence:

> It is the essence of these religious groups, and of their right to establish tribunals for the decision of questions arising among

themselves, that those decisions should be binding in all cases of ecclesiastical cognizance, subject only to such appeals as the organism itself provides for.[2]

As we shall see, however, in one of the most important of all mediating structures in our American life—the schools—both educational liberty *and* the liberty of churches are threatened. If all education becomes state-dictated, we will have destroyed the mediating structure that is the absolute keystone of our entire structure of human liberty.

The Religious School as a Mediating Structure

A nonpublic school is a mediating structure in several ways. For many parents, it is, next to the family itself, the chief area in which parents exercise what the Supreme Court recognizes as their "primary role" of bringing up their children.[3] They exercise that primary role but not directly in day-to-day instruction (though some parents do undertake to educate their children in the home—a matter which involves constitutional and other considerations not relevant here). Instead, they exercise their right in the important matter of choosing a school, an issue in *Wisconsin* v. *Yoder,* a case involving the rights of Amish parents. Although some statist lawyers attempt to pass off *Yoder* as an offbeat decision on an ancient and unique social phenomenon, the Court looked upon the Amish very differently. It carefully scrutinized the Amish parents who took the stand at the trial, seeing them not as characters in a costume play, but as twentieth century parents seeking liberty—liberty of education for their children in a way that parental conscience demanded. Their way was indeed different from what the state of Wisconsin required, different, too, from what the community of New Glarus, Wisconsin, believed was best for them. It was in fact an education that did not even involve schooling, as most understand that term. Here is what the Court had to say:

> But in this case, the Amish have introduced persuasive evidence undermining the arguments the State has advanced to support its claims in terms of the welfare of the child and society as a whole. The record strongly indicates that accommodating the religious objections of the Amish by forgoing one, or at most two, additional years of compulsory education will not impair the physical or mental health of the child, or result in an in-

---

[2] Serbian Eastern Orthodox Diocese v. Milivojevich, 426 U.S. 696, 49L. Ed. 2d. 151, 164 (1976).

[3] Wisconsin v. Yoder, 406 U.S. 205, 232 (1972).

ability to be self-supporting or to discharge the duties and responsibilities of citizenship, or in any other way materially detract from the welfare of society.[4]

Parents are one factor in the private school's role as a mediating structure; children are another for it may be in private schooling that the child's opportunity to experience what is best for him in education is realized. The child's right here is a sort of derivative right exercised for him by the parent. He can have an educational experience distinct from the state's program and linked, because of parental choice and perhaps religion, to the family. In *Yoder,* Justice Douglas, in his separate opinion, fretted over whether the Amish children's rights had really been protected. On the stand, they had been fair game for the prosecution, which wisely chose not to match wits with such innocent and well-spoken witnesses. They were put on the stand, however, not to espouse "child rights" independently of parental rights, but to show that they were well fulfilled and happy, thanks to the distinctive nonstate education that is the Amish way.

When the factor of religion is introduced into this mediating structure, we see the structure at its maximum importance. The religious school uniquely enables religious parents and children to know, love, and serve God. Thus it is indispensable to the free and full exercise of religion. Let those who press for government regulation of religious schools, or who would manipulate the tax structure to starve them out, note that well. And let those who quail in the face of such threats, or who would secularize these schools in return for public aid, note it well.

Finally, the *religious* school is a mediating structure because it manifests (sometimes heroically) the religious faith of a community. The community consists of the believers, or church, whose faith and whose sacrifices bring the school into being. The school would not exist except as an extension, and expression, of the religious community. Of course, if it begins to see itself as a secular endeavor with religious aspects, it has not only lost its soul but is no longer a mediating structure. Instead of enabling religious freedom in the presence of the state, it becomes a promoter of state ends, to which it is willing to subordinate the religious aspect.

Government Assaults on Religious Schools

I have implied that, in the face of the present assault on mediating structures, their natural protectors appear to have taken flight. In the case of

---

[4] Ibid., 234.

private schools, there are many instances. Looking only at the federal assault, we see, for example, the Department of Health, Education, and Welfare's Title IX Guidelines on sex discrimination. These preposterous departures from statute forbade a school to dismiss a student from its education program on the basis of her "pregnancy, childbirth, false pregnancy, termination of pregnancy."[5] The worst thing about the Title IX Guidelines, however, was not their substance but the reaction to that substance. It would hardly be correct to say that private educational groups (including major religious groups) got in line; rather, they led the parade. They promptly sent out detailed memoranda to their memberships on how to comply. Apparently, no one bothered to ask those legally obvious questions which ought to come naturally to citizens of a free society: Did Congress give HEW power to impose all these specific requirements? and, if it did, did the Congress act within our Constitution?

The federal census bureau has circulated to religious schools throughout the nation Form CB-82, marked "Census of Service Industries." The form demands that seminaries and other church entities furnish the government with statistics on their total annual 1977 payroll, 1977 operating receipts, and/or total revenue. This is odd. The statute cited as the authority for this remarkable exploration of religious institutions by the Commerce Department is 13 United States Code, Section 131, which requires the secretary of commerce to take censuses of "manufactures, of mineral industries, and of other businesses, including the distributive trades, service establishments, and transportation. . . ." Again, major religious groups jumped through the government's hoop. They saw no need to fuss over churches being classed as "businesses." Moreover, they feared that if they did make a fuss, the public servants might *really* get tough.

I could cite many other examples of current governmental assaults upon private religious schools and other religious endeavors, and of the seeming eagerness of religious representatives to accept the intrusions. One can only guess why. Perhaps it is the pathetic desire, so evident today among leaders of once-religious colleges, to be part of the "mainstream." Fear is another reason—the fear of appearances or other misplaced fears. Those who fear the evils in which American public servants may indulge doggedly observe the motto, "Don't make waves!" I will not respond at length to such attitudes, beyond reminding the image-conscious that the highest calling may sometimes consist in moving from the mainstream of contemporary fad to the mountaintop of principle and

---

[5] 40 *Federal Register,* 24128 "Nondiscrimination on Basis of Sex," 86.40 (June 4, 1973).

integrity and telling the fearful that we are not yet citizens of a people's republic and that we do *not* have to live by sufferance of public servants.

Resistance to Assault

There is also a picture of resistance, and it is a glowing one. In a series of litigations now in the courts, mediating educational structures which have come under attack are engaged in a vigorous counterattack. (Because of my involvement in some of these cases, I cannot go into them here as fully as I would like.) These are cases on the cutting edge of civil liberty in education, and how they ultimately turn out will have close bearing on how free our people will be in the future.

One group of cases involves governmental aid to children attending private religious schools. The children receive aid upon the premises of these schools. Several organizations have challenged this in court, contending that it constitutes an establishment of religion forbidden by the First Amendment. In their view, the main effect of the aid programs is to advance religion; they also claim that it creates excessive entanglements between church and state. These familiar arguments have achieved success in Supreme Court decisions, which have held that most of the workable and practical forms of aid to children in religious schools are barred by the Establishment Clause. Five justices of the present Court seem to think that the Founding Fathers would not have approved of using a publicly owned bus to provide a field trip for children in a religious school which meets compulsory attendance requirements if the school teacher chooses the destination. Justice Blackmun said that "it is the individual teacher who makes the trip meaningful" and "where the teacher works within and for a sectarian institution, an unacceptable risk of fostering of religion is an inevitable by-product."[6] Here the Court once again views the sectarian school teacher as an automaton, an image it first presented to the nation in *Lemon* v. *Kurtzman,* 403 U.S. 602 (1971). The teacher may be renowned for her professionalism, the court says, but within a religious school she is psychologically incapable of being religiously neutral. So, although the statute is designed "to enrich the secular studies of students," and although the teacher is both intelligent and law-abiding, on a field trip she will compulsively convert the countryside into a maze of religious objects and willy-nilly direct the bus driver to the nearest shrine.[7] That is the present Court's view of the Establishment Clause with

---

[6] Wolman v. Walter, 433 U.S. 229, 53L. Ed. 2d, 714, 736 (1977).

[7] In Meek v. Pittenger, 421 U.S. 349 (1973), the trial record disclosed the testimony of a Lutheran child psychologist who was hired by the state to provide psychological services in nonpublic (including Catholic) schools. His sworn testimony showed him

regard to these cases. If we go against that view and argue that the services in question are good for children, how should we defend them?

There is only one theory of defense that is compatible with religious liberty, and it is as follows: (a) the Free Exercise Clause of the First Amendment guarantees the right to have a child educated in a religious school; (b) the Constitution protects the parents' right to choose the form of education they want for their child; (c) most parents today are oppressed by excessive taxation and inflation and cannot actually exercise those rights without some economic accommodation by government; (d) the programs benefit children; (e) because they entail aid to religious institutions in only an indirect and minimal way, the Free Exercise Clause considerations vastly outweigh Establishment Clause considerations. In other words, government is constitutionally obligated to accommodate Free Exercise and parental choice.

Amazingly, instead of that defense, a wholly different theory has been proposed, namely, that the religious schools are not "narrowly sectarian," that they are in fact so religiously "neutral" that they can be aided with public funds within the strictures laid down by the Supreme Court in the prior cases denying aid—indeed, within the aforementioned bizarre doctrine on field trips. This "defense" of certain programs throws away the real defense of religious liberty. Proclaiming that religious schools are "neutral" denies the true nature of those schools and would bargain off integrity in return for public aid.

In a second group of cases, the government, through the National Labor Relations Board, has attempted to regulate employment relationships in private religious schools. The first targets were Catholic schools, which have numerous employees. At the outset, a number of those schools capitulated to NLRB demands. Justifying their surrender on hazily stated grounds of "social justice" and the "inevitability" of government success, oblivious to the inheritance which was theirs to protect, and blind to the real significance of NLRB demands, the schools helped build crippling precedents for other Catholic schools which, to the contrary, had a high vision of themselves and their liberties and were willing to fight for freedom.

Ignoring these precedents, some schools decided to resist in court.

---

a competent professional who considered himself bound by the code of ethics of the American Psychological Association *not* to introduce religion into his services. In the face of the record six justices held that, once he crossed the premises of the religious school, "the potential for (his) impermissible fostering of religion . . . is nonetheless present." *Id*. at 371. The Court did not make it clear whether the Catholic school would beam Catholic notions at him or he would beam Lutheran notions at the children. The record showed that neither had happened. But the six justices were dead sure that one or both would.

In the Diocese of Gary, Indiana, the bishop took the NLRB to court, and in the Archdiocese of Philadelphia, five pastors of parish schools sued the NLRB and secured an injunction against that body. The Supreme Court agreed to consider the question of NLRB jurisdiction over religious schools in its next term. At stake in the NLRB litigation are the Free Exercise of Religion rights of religious schools. These cases are not merely cases of governmental entanglements with these schools; at a more profound level is the question of what constitutes "religion" within the meaning of the First Amendment. The government contends that the Catholic schools are "only partly religious." If this mischievous idea were accepted by the Supreme Court, a truly secularist view of religion would be established in American constitutional law—the "religion of the sacristy," to borrow the phrase borrowed by John Courtney Murray. That is the kind of religion that the constitutions of various people's republics provide for. From Roger Williams to Jesse Jackson, it is unknown in our free tradition.

There is a third group of cases that are perhaps the most significant of all. It involves fundamentalist Christian schools, which are trying to survive state attack. These schools have managed thus far to resist successfully the efforts directed against them. In three of the four chief cases that have come to the courts, the attack on the schools took the form of criminal prosecution of parents whose children attended non-state-approved schools; in a fourth case, the state brought an injunction against the schools themselves. Two of the cases (*Ohio* v. *Whisner* and *Vermont* v. *LaBarge*[8]) resulted in victory for the parents.[9]

Maximum governmental pressure has been applied to these fundamentalist schools, which are true "mediating structures." In three cases, in fact, the pressure consisted of criminal prosecutions. In the fourth case, where an injunction was sought, the state made pointed reference to its compulsory attendance statute under which criminal proceedings may be brought. One wonders, Why the pressure? If people must pay fines or go to jail because they choose particular schools for their children, the schools themselves face doom. What sort of schools must these be, that they must be run out of business? one asks. Surely they must be places of disease or physical danger, or schools of vice or subversion, or frauds

---

[8] State of Ohio v. Whisner, et al., 47 Ohio St. 2d 181 (1976); State of Vermont v. LaBarge, et al., 134 Vt. 276 (1976).

[9] Editor's note: in a related case, the trial court in Hinton v. Kentucky Board of Education ruled in favor of the plaintiff, limiting the jurisdiction of the state over church schools. The decision is on appeal. In North Carolina v. Columbia Christian Academy, the trial court set aside some late regulations imposed on the academy and upheld others. Both parties have appealed.

which take tuition from people and then turn out incompetents, illiterates, or non-law-abiding graduates.

When confronted with the facts, however, we find that the schools are decent places—safe, sanitary, and not racially segregated. The children are well mannered and happy. They have learned to pray and to love God, neighbor, and country—that is obvious. They speak and read English. They test well in nationally standardized basic skills tests. Their parents are law-abiding folk, and the children promise to be. When one becomes familiar with these schools, one finds they are true mediating structures—few and small, admittedly (though growing). They are a locus in which people realize a way of life and fulfill hopes for their children. Thus, they *enable* freedom. Why the pressure? One can but guess.

There is, of course, the "government-as-industry" point to which I have alluded. There is also, however, an undeniable *animus* which helps fuel these cases—a righteousness without being right. After all, the fundamentalists are often vulnerable—few in number, few of wealth. Perhaps powerlessness attracts harshness. Again, it may be that public servants, who remain prudently silent about major corruptions, are relieved to be able to denounce evil when it consists of resistance to a petty regulation by one who has no political friends.

Another factor which may propel great state exertions against these innocent people is money. Back of the public schools lies a vast industry. Public schools are declining in population and approbation. The industries producing bricks, cement, furniture, plumbing, air conditioning, and equipment gain when a public school is built; they lose when building declines. Then there are the book industry and the electronic media manufacturers. Nonpublic schools often use old buildings and (good) old books. If they build, it is inexpensively, and they buy with frugality. There are other money factors (the loss of state reimbursement to school districts when nonpublic schools are established) and the job factor. Nonpublic schools absorb child populations which would otherwise afford the basis for hiring teachers and administrators, and maintaining public schools.

Perhaps these factors help to explain the hysteria which routinely greets resistance to state absorption of nonpublic schools or the affording of relief to nonpublic school parents or aid to their children. Public school leaders, lobbyists, and attorneys—in states in which more than 50 percent of all state moneys go to public education—then, with histrionics rarely seen outside of Verdi operas, predict the imminent and cataclysmic doom of the public school.

What may we expect in most of the court cases in which mediating structures are now fighting for their existence? Attorneys who predict litigation outcomes for clients usually speak foolishly. What we may expect in these cases can only be seen in light of the basic test which the Supreme Court has laid down for those cases in which the state seeks to restrict personal liberty: "The State may prevail only upon showing a subordinating interest which is compelling."[10] Thus, the mediating structures must put the state to the test, not vice versa. Government must be made to show precisely how the interests it asserts are compellingly superior to the healthful, innocent, and freedom-accommodating life of a mediating structure. While the mediating structure must demonstrate the reality of its constitutional claim, it must never, in its own defense, strike its colors, depart from principle, settle for less than true liberty. If penalties and prisons may be its immediate reward, freedom for our posterity may be its ultimate gift.

---

[10] Bates v. City of Little Rock, 361 U.S. 516, 524 (1960).

The School as a Mediating Structure: Some Concerns about Subversion and Co-optation

Donald A. Erickson

This is an analysis, somewhat speculative, of mediating structures, defined by Peter Berger and Richard John Neuhaus as "those institutions standing between the individual in his private life and the large institutions of public life." Like Berger and Neuhaus, I am concerned about loss of community and the strong and growing "animus against government, bureaucracy, and bigness as such." I am worried about "megastructures, . . . the growing bureaucracies that administer wide sectors of the society, such as . . . education and the organized professions." I see megastructures as "typically alienating, . . . not helpful, in providing meaning and identity for individual existence." I lament the loss of "the little platoon we belong to in society."[1]

Like Franklin H. Littell, I am alarmed at a "basic disjarment between the [human] . . . and his ground of being, both toward nature and toward the social matrix," a dislocation that creates "personal and social despair." Like Franklin Littell, I consider the liberal attempt to "free" men from the "biasing," "provincial" structures of religion, ethnicity, locality, and the like, as "one of the most torturous enterprises of modern culture."[2] Similarly, Robert Alter speaks of "all the forces that seem subtly or crudely to coerce the self."[3] But, strangely, as Leonard Fein notes, many liberals overlook or ignore evidence that participation in relatively small, cohesive enterprises is essential, for most people, for a sense of identity and for the ability to relate humanely to others.[4]

So much for my testimonial. Now for the analysis. I will attempt to

---

Dr. Erickson teaches at the University of San Francisco.

[1] Peter L. Berger and Richard John Neuhaus, *To Empower People: The Role of Mediating Structures in Public Policy* (Washington, D.C.: American Enterprise Institute for Public Policy Research, 1977), pp. 2, 4.

[2] Franklin H. Littell, "Sectarian Protestantism and the Pursuit of Wisdom: Must Technological Objectives Prevail?" in Donald A. Erickson, ed., *Public Controls for Nonpublic Schools* (Chicago: University of Chicago Press, 1969), p. 70.

[3] Robert Alter, "A Fever of Ethnicity," *Commentary* 53 (June, 1972), p. 68.

[4] Leonard Fein, "The Limits of Universalism," in Henry J. Levin, ed., *Community Control of Schools* (Washington, D.C.: Brookings Institution, 1970), pp. 89, 90.

describe how a mediating structure (one type, at least) functions, some conditions that enable it to flourish, and how it may be subverted or co-opted—even transformed into a megastructure—"by the government in a too eager embrace."[5] Forgive me if I focus specifically on the school, the only institution I know much about. In describing the school as a mediating structure, I believe I am illustrating general tendencies. These tendencies may be evident in other sectors of our economic, political, and cultural life.

The Basic Idea of the School as a Mediating Structure

While acknowledging the need to establish the historical point more conclusively than space permits here, I begin with the contention that the school (elementary and secondary, but particularly the former) in the United States started, in both its public and its private manifestations, as a mediating structure, one of those people-sized, empowering, value-generating, value-maintaining "little aggregations" that stand between the often-faceless state and the often-threatened individual.

The most important distinguishing features of the mediating structure I am about to depict are that it provides the individual with a sense of power (the opposite of alienation, in Melvin Seeman's terms[6]); with a sense of belonging to a like-minded, cohesive group; with a strongly believed-in goal that is bigger than self; and with a sense of being needed, at times approaching the perception of being indispensable. Also, though this feature is not shown in my diagram (figure 1), the structure is people-sized. Thus, if I may repeat myself, it is a people-sized, empowering, value-generating, value-maintaining "little aggregation" that stands the often-faceless state and the often-threatened individual. To use a shorthand term, the mediating structure provides the individual with some of the conditions, at least, of self-actualization.

With only minor modifications, it is possible to transform each one of the components of this simple depiction of a mediating structure into a slightly more elaborate description of a school (figure 2). We may view the obvious need for altruistic help (component a) as arising from institutional jeopardy—the sense that the enterprise (in this case, the school) is fragile, or endangered, or likely to collapse unless the individual provides altruistic assistance. The strongly believed-in goal, bigger than self (component b), becomes the school's special, focused mission, clearly perceived and agreed upon, and important because it affects the life

---

[5] Berger and Neuhaus, p. 7.
[6] Melvin Seeman, "On the Meaning of Alienation," *American Sociological Review* 24 (1959), p. 784.

FIGURE 1

MAJOR PSYCHO-SOCIOLOGICAL CONTRIBUTIONS OF THE MEDIATING
STRUCTURE TO SELF-ACTUALIZATION

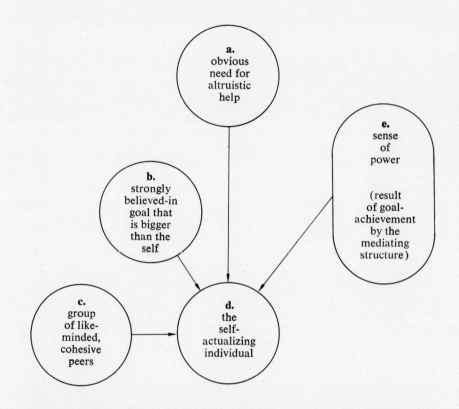

chances of one's children. The like-minded, cohesive peers, who give the
individual a group to which to belong (component c), become a homogeneous and cohesive entity as school clients. The sense of power arising
out of goal-achievement by the mediating structure (component e) is
seen now in more specific terms, arising from successful teaching-learning
encounters in the school the individual has done so much to establish
and/or preserve. The self-actualizing individual (component d) becomes, of course, the parent with the group to belong to, with the goal
bigger than self, with the sense of being needed intensely, and with the
consciousness that the enterprise to which the effort has been devoted is
successful. To paraphrase perhaps with too broad a sweep, what I take
to be the major point of the Berger-Neuhaus monograph, one does not

FIGURE 2

A HIGHLY SIMPLIFIED REPRESENTATION OF THE SCHOOL AS A MEDIATING STRUCTURE

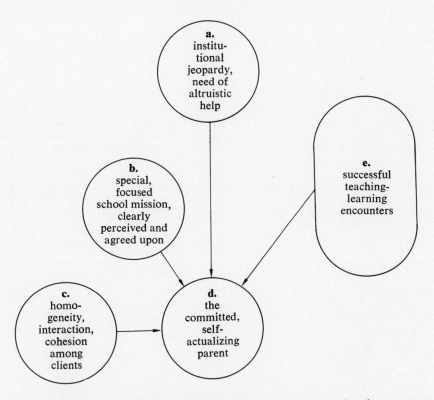

obtain these immensely rewarding conditions mere by voting for a member of Congress, or by purchasing an item in a department store. Hence, the need for mediating structures.

If we shift our representation of the school as mediating structure only slightly (figure 3), we produce a more dynamic model. We may use the model to discuss in some detail the causal relationships that make the structure work (please ignore for the moment the numbers assigned to the arrows). Schools approaching the conditions of this model embody the assumption that sentiments and interpersonal relationships are at least as important (to school productivity and to individual self-actualization) as is either the technical competence of teachers or the diversity of human composition and ideological thrust of the schools. The type of

FIGURE 3

SEMI-ELABORATED MODEL OF THE SCHOOL AS A MEDIATING
STRUCTURE (OR GEMEINSCHAFT)

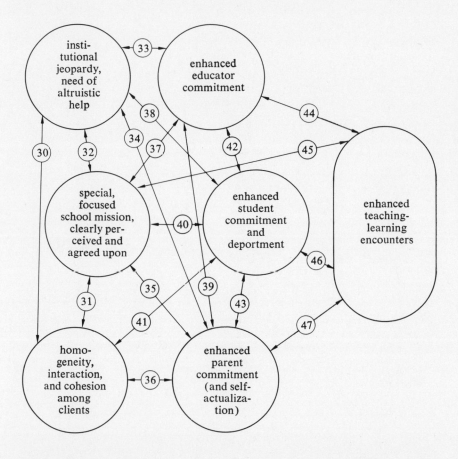

school described here might well be described as a *Gemeinschaft* (community) rather than a *Gesellschaft* (society). The former approximates the close-knit relationships of the extended family; the latter, like many modern schools, may be described in terms of the segmental, superficial interactions of people rambling around a department store on a Saturday afternoon.[7]

---

[7] That is precisely the term Cusick uses to describe a modern high school. Where students are massed and undifferentiated, there is little more than superficial student-teacher interaction, little truly rewarding recognition of achievement, only surface

To elucidate just a few distinguishing characteristics of the *Gemein-schaft,* or mediating structure, school, I will refer from this point onward to relationships suggested by my recent research in collaboration with Richard Nault, though our evidence must be regarded as still very tentative.[8] As a way of simplifying the discussion, I will talk almost exclusively of commitment, assuming that everyone knows, given the passages above, that I am at least equally concerned about self-actualization. Commitment and self-actualization are very closely related. It is difficult to conceive of high commitment in a situation providing little opportunity to self-actualize.

Institutional Jeopardy. In schools, as in other settings, one of the most gratifying human experiences is to feel needed by, or even virtually indispensable to, an enterprise with worthy goals. This sensation may elicit more commitment still, if one seems to be doing something that requires unusual nobility of character. The probability that these feelings and perceptions will occur should increase when people sense that the enterprise to which they are contributing time, talent, and energy is seriously jeopardized (arrows 33, 34, and 38 in figure 3). Teachers and parents say their commitment to a school is enhanced when they feel strongly needed, and there is evidence that students may experience a similar reaction.[9] Some Canadian teachers, for example, have declared that they feel better working in Catholic schools with low salaries (that is, privately supported Catholic schools in British Columbia and Manitoba) than in Catholic schools with high salaries (publicly supported Catholic schools in Alberta, Saskatchewan, and Ontario). High salaries, in these cases, signify that a teacher, much like a cog in a machine, can be replaced, while the low salaries are a symbol of special devoted service that few people are willing to provide.[10] Other teachers speak of the benefits of understaffing in meagerly supported schools. When barely enough people are available to handle all vital duties, it appears that staff members value each other's contributions more highly, and express their mutual appreciation more often or more intensely, thus reinforcing commitment. The

student involvement, and a notable fragmentation of experience. Philip A. Cusick, *Inside High School: The Student's World* (New York: Holt, Rinehart and Winston, 1973).

[8] Donald A. Erickson and Richard L. Nault, *Currency, Choice, and Commitment: An Exploratory Study of the Effects of Public Money and Related Regulation on Canadian Catholic Schools* (San Francisco: Center for Research on Private Education, University of San Francisco, January 1978).

[9] *Ibid.*

[10] *Ibid.*

pattern is reminiscent of the apparent effects on student commitment of "undermanning" in the extracurricular activities of small high schools.[11]

Special, Focused School Mission. There have been many complaints in the recent literature about diffuse, all-encompassing public school goals (since public schools often seem expected to compensate for virtually all of society's ills) and about the strident disagreements among public school clients over what schools should attempt to accomplish.[12] When clients do agree on school goals, energy otherwise expended on seeking consensus, and trying to manage conflicts, or achieve contradictory objectives simultaneously can be channelled, instead, into more productive activities. When goals are more consistent and clearly focused, they should be more readily achievable, even if the energy available remains constant (arrow 45). Under these conditions, schools should encourage student learning more efficiently; clients, believing the school is sensitive to their wishes, should respond with enhanced commitment (arrow 47), and students should respond positively when they experience more positive outcomes from teaching-learning encounters (arrow 46).

Group Norms and the Need to Reciprocate. Teachers have reported that they feel more obliged to pour themselves into their work when they perceive that parents are unusually committed to a school. Similarly, parents have spoken of their need to reciprocate when teachers seem highly dedicated (arrow 39).[13] It seems likely that most students are compelled to respond with enhanced commitment and deportment when teachers (arrow 42) or parents (arrow 43) appear to be giving their all to a school. Conversely, it is difficult to believe that the commitment of teachers and parents is unaffected by the attitudes and behavior of students.

The client homogeneity mentioned earlier may foster cohesive client groups, especially when parents have the opportunity to interact extensively. The groups may develop norms of high commitment (arrow 36) and belief systems, reinforcing the perception that a school offers special benefits and thus deserves committed support (arrows 31 and 35). The influences of client groups may well extend to students (arrow

---

[11] R. G. Barker and P. V. Gump, *Big School, Small School* (Stanford: Stanford University Press, 1968).

[12] See, for example, Decker F. Walker, "The Structure of Goals, Knowledge, and Curricula in Schooling" (paper prepared for the National Institute of Education's National Invitational Conference on School Organization and Effects, San Diego, January 27–29, 1978), pp. 48–49.

[13] Erickson and Nault, *Currency, Choice, and Commitment.*

41). One would expect flourishing, cohesive, homogeneous groups to provide special rewards and inducements to their members and to the teachers who serve them, such as a sense of belonging, of being highly regarded for contributing, and of being better than the outsiders who do not work in, or patronize, the school. Schools characterized by such groups must surely seem special (arrow 31). They must be singularly attractive to people whose aspirations are congruent with their special characteristics. Teachers and administrators must feel obliged to respond to the sense of special mission and clarity of school goals (arrow 37), and to the unusual parent commitment (arrow 39). As the commitment of these educators rises, parents must tend to reciprocate.

Close Links between School and Home and Other Community Institutions. Close links between school and home and between school and other community institutions not shown in the diagrams may be an important aspect of the school as a mediating structure. Visiting schools that are extensively meshed with homes (some small public schools in Amish communities, for example), I have been convinced that this link has a powerful impact, both upon teaching-learning encounters and upon the self-actualization of the people who devote themselves so wholeheartedly to this "little aggregation." Levels of stress and anxiety seem remarkably low. The teacher is not merely the incumbent of a particular role, but is an individual drawn from a close-knit community, possessing intimate knowledge of each child's idiosyncracies and family history. Parents are extensively involved in school affairs. Since the school is quite obviously an extension of the home and reinforces the values of the parents, parents seem powerfully committed to the school.

Some private schools may enjoy special advantages in this connection. In available descriptions of traditional parochial schools, it seems obvious that the close connection between school and parish church is a source of strong parent commitment to the school, for the school is then important, not only in its own right, but as an arm of the church.[14] There is much symbolic importance in the fact, moreover, that the school building may become more central to parish activities as a whole than will the church building. Another advantage of close links between school and church may be that school personnel often benefit from *two* bases of authority—their roles in the school and their roles in the church.

Close ties among school, church, and home may also enhance par-

---

[14] Joseph H. Fichter, *Parochial School: A Sociological Study* (Notre Dame, Ind.: University of Notre Dame Press, 1958); James W. Sanders, *The Education of an Urban Minority: Catholics in Chicago, 1833–1965* (New York: Oxford University Press, 1976).

ent commitment by strengthening the client-group norms and collective belief systems mentioned earlier. Having both the school and the church in common, the clients interact more extensively.

Enhanced Teaching-Learning Encounters. The apparent success of a mediating structure school in achieving its goals is not only a product but also a cause of commitment and sense of power on the part of parents, students, and teachers. It is perfectly obvious, I suspect, that most parents are gratified to see their children blossom, especially as a consequence of extensive parental contributions to a school, and that students are "turned on" by success in the classroom. In what I regard as the most definitive work on teachers, Dan C. Lortie demonstrates that they, too, derive powerful psychic rewards from teaching-learning encounters.[15] According to Lortie, the act of teaching itself provides the rewards teachers have traditionally valued the most (arrow 44), but does so in a discouragingly unpredictable fashion. One would expect, then, that any school factors which increase the frequency or intensity of rewards derived from the teaching-learning encounter would enhance teacher commitment. These commitment-inducing factors probably include selective student admissions (not in the diagrams), focused goals (arrows 40 and 46), and other arrangements, perhaps peculiar to schools as mediating structures, that contribute to student commitment (arrows 38, 40, 41, 42, and 43).

The Subversion of Public Schools

We are now in a position to examine the possibility that public schools, which I think were primarily mediating structures to begin with, have been subverted in that regard. Virtually all of them, I suspect, have been seriously debilitated as commitment-inducing "little aggregations," and many, especially in our big cities, have been transmuted into mega-structures.

In early America, the nascent counterpart of the modern public school was generally meagerly funded and subject to the vagaries of local finance. Quite visible financial sacrifices were often involved. People had to "pitch in" in many ways to keep the school going. Often teachers were remunerated partly by the device of "living around" from home to home in the community. Until very recent years, the adjective "underpaid" was habitually attached to the noun "teacher," and as Lortie's evidence shows, remnants of the dedicatory ethic are still not entirely gone from

---

[15] Dan C. Lortie, *Schoolteacher: A Sociological Study* (Chicago: University of Chicago Press, 1975).

the nation's classrooms.[16] In the light of the special working conditions that teachers enjoy, and in the wake of several years of militant collective bargaining, it is no longer obvious that teachers are underpaid. Public school systems seldom seem seriously underfinanced or understaffed, except to educators. Teachers, with greater financial rewards than ever, are accused of exhibiting less commitment than ever. Parents tell us their commitment is reduced because they no longer feel needed by their tax-supported schools. Funds are available to purchase needed services, and unions are not enthusiastic about volunteer labor. Such, briefly, are some unanticipated side-effects of improved school funding. If an obvious need for altruistic help is an important characteristic of a mediating structure, the decline of these people-empowering entities is partly attributable to public money. When there is a guaranteed flow of dollars to purchase all necessary services, and when ten applicants are waiting to take each vacated job, people generally feel neither essential to an enterprise nor empowered by the awareness that their efforts make an essential difference.

It would be misleading to suggest, however, that all public schools are now megastructures. Many public schools still seem an integral part of their immediate neighborhoods, still project an aura of being in some sense special, still manage to focus their goals to some extent, still (by virtue of neighborhood homogeneity) feature relatively cohesive, like-minded client groups, still appear to maintain good instruction, and still, by one means or another, convince parents that at least some assistance is needed from them. My point is simply that maintaining these *Gemein-schaft* characteristics is more and more difficult in public schools, and in a good many situations has become impossible.

A major diminution of the role of public schools as mediating structures was effected when experts in many fields, during the Progressive era, usurped the authority of common citizens. In numerous respects, in fact, the Progressive era was a revolt against the "parochial," "disunifying" influences of such mediating structures as neighborhoods and ethnic groups.[17] Experts promised, in effect, to recast the provincial attitudes of the citizenry, making them more compatible with the requirements of a modern technological society. Experts would convert private wants into a public spirit and public interest. Professionalism would bring a new respect for rational discussion rather than pressure-group politics into such arenas as education. The movement was abetted, to be sure, by the virtual takeover of school systems in many cities by political machines.

---

[16] *Ibid.*

[17] Rush Welter, *Popular Education and Popular Thought in America* (New York: Columbia University Press, 1962), pp. 263–266.

The net result, however, was a restructuring of public schools to disempower common citizens and to empower educational experts.[18]

The likelihood that public schools would function as mediating structures was diminished further, especially after World War II, when the apostles of economies of scale produced the national transformation known as school reorganization and consolidation.[19] The schoolhouse at the country crossroads virtually disappeared, its students bused to the nearest school in town. Small school districts were melded into large and often enormous ones. The size alone of many American schools now makes it difficult, if not impossible, to maintain *Gemeinschaft*. As for our massive urban school systems governed from downtown, which of them is structured to give citizens a sense of identity, power, usefulness, belonging, or responsibility?

American schools are now governed by boards presiding over an impossible agglomerate of competing, dissentious communities, demanding an often-contradictory, unfocused grocery-list of school accomplishments. Students drawn from an extreme diversity of home backgrounds are difficult to process in any single institution, often reacting so badly that classrooms are beleaguered and teachers suffer battle fatigue. Everyone's commitment suffers. The effectiveness of teaching-learning encounters is reduced as a consequence of attenuated commitment and lack of clear goals. In reaction to reduced school productivity, commitment drops still more. And, as if to defeat any efforts to regenerate *Gemeinschaft* in local schools with high motives but little attention to drastic side-effects, we bus students away from their neighborhoods, further weakening links between school and home.

These analyses are admittedly simplified. Many causes not reflected in my diagrams and discussion contribute to the malaise in many public schools. I contend, however, that the shift from mediating structure toward megastructure, and from *Gemeinschaft* to *Gesellschaft,* is one of the most destructive developments of all. I believe, furthermore, that much current strength in private schools is best characterized as a reaction against public school megastructures—as an attempt to recapture the *Gemeinschaft* relationships represented in figure 3. Despite this strength, however, private schools are an endangered species. They are intensely, increasingly jeopardized by a "double taxation" policy and other government-imposed handicaps.

---

[18] L. Harmon Zeigler, Harvey J. Tucker, and L. A. Wilson, "How School Control Was Wrested from the People," *Phi Delta Kappan* 58 (March 1977), 534–539.

[19] For a general overview of the movement, see Leslie L. Chisholm, *School District Reorganization* (Chicago: Midwest Administration Center, University of Chicago, 1957).

The Co-optation of Private (and Public) Schools

I have suggested some mechanisms that seem primarily responsible for the subversion of our erstwhile mediating structure, the public schools. My analysis would not be complete, however, without a discussion of the effects of existing public policy, and certain possible changes in that policy, on private schools. Some of these policy effects are relevant, in generally overlooked ways, for public schools as well. It is conceivable that the nation will end up destroying all *Gemeinschaft* schools, first by subverting public schools, through the means discussed earlier, and second, by co-opting private schools.

In figure 4, I suggest a complex set of relationships, only a few of which may be explicated here, that link public policy in four issue-areas (see boxes A through D along the left side of figure 4) to the *Gemeinschaft* or mediating structure phenomena discussed earlier. The diagram is based on some recent research with private schools, but it is relevant as well, in several respects, to forces that have subverted public schools. It may be important to discuss several ways, suggested in the diagram, in which the major features of mediating structures may be attenuated or obliterated by government.

Programmatic Controls. I have argued extensively elsewhere that government may require everything it is entitled to demand of private schools without specifying how the requisite student outcomes are produced.[20] If it is demonstrably necessary for all future citizens to learn to read at a specified level of competence, for example, the art of testing is sufficiently advanced to determine whether this objective has been accomplished. Even a cursory examination of state school codes makes clear, however, that government has a lamentable tendency to regulate the *manner* in which schools must function (I call such regulation "programmatic") rather than the *results* schools must achieve. In another paper at this conference, William B. Ball discusses the alarming current trend in some states to prosecute as criminals parents whose deep convictions compel them to patronize schools which government bureaucracies are unwilling to approve. The special modes of teacher recruitment, selection, training, placement, supervision, and motivation common in many private schools in the past are more than tangentially related, I think, to several important factors discussed earlier, such as close links between home and church (arrow 6), institutional jeopardy (arrow 16), and a sense of special school mission (arrow 18). These mechanisms could easily be displaced by

---

[20] Erickson, *Public Controls for Non-Public Schools.*

71

72

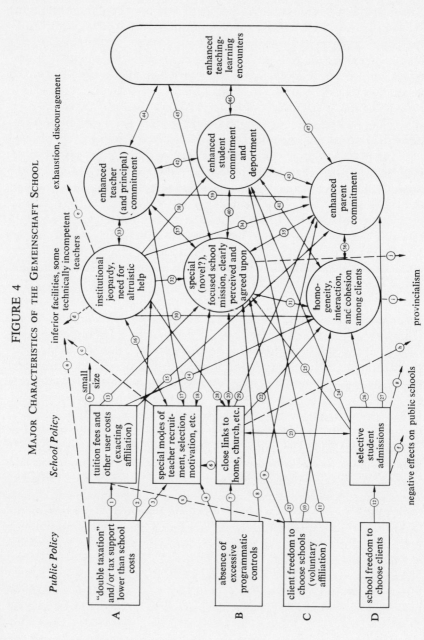

FIGURE 4

MAJOR CHARACTERISTICS OF THE GEMEINSCHAFT SCHOOL

demands for teacher certification, when one considers what certification typically involves (arrow 7). More importantly, the exceptionally extensive regulations that numerous states are now attempting to impose on private schools could so thoroughly obliterate the distinguishing characteristics of these schools that they would have no reason to exist any longer (arrow 8). In fact, both public and private schools are subverted from their erstwhile functions as mediating structures when more and more discretion is taken from the local level and lodged elsewhere—in state bureaucracies, in federal money-giving agencies, and in distant state and federal courtrooms. The intentions behind centralization and nationalization are often noble, but the results are often alienating to the common citizen. It does not surprise me at all that many citizens in many parts of the country no longer regard the local public schools as *theirs* in any significant sense. Many state agencies apparently are working hard to produce the same coercive effects in private schools.

Growing "Double Taxation" Handicaps. Since most patrons of private schools must "pay twice" for their children's instruction, once through public school taxation and once through user costs at private schools, it is obvious that private schools, though constitutionally guaranteed the "right" to exist, may be put out of business through economic coercion. Although this point probably needs no elaboration here, it is one of the most basic, pervasive realities in the world of education today. In the light of the constitutional constraints, the nation could easily lose most of its private schools, along with the important functions they perform as mediating structures, because there is no way of alleviating the financial pressure.

Carelessly Designed Financial Support. Our above-mentioned research suggests (though not yet conclusively) that, by granting Catholic schools virtually the same tax support as public schools, thus removing the need for client fees and donated services (arrow 1), Canadian provinces such as Alberta, Saskatchewan, and Ontario may have done much to attenuate parent commitment (arrows 13, 14, 15, 35, and 36).[21] When a school is fully supported by taxation, clients need assume no significant burdens to affiliate; affiliation may be described as lax (not exacting). Under conditions of lax affiliation, one would expect clients to weigh differences among schools less deliberately, and to affiliate with less commitment, than when affiliation is exacting. Clients may view schools which appear to cost them nothing as offering nothing special and thus warranting no

---

[21] Erickson and Nault, *Currency, Choice, and Commitment.*

special effort. They may assume that if a school exacts no significant costs, it offers no unusual benefits. Conscious of no notable investment, they may feel no need to work toward a significant payoff. Conversely, exactitude in client affiliation may enhance both client commitment and the perception that the school is distinctive (arrows 13, 14). Noting the extra costs of patronizing a school not supported (partially or fully) by taxes, potential clients who expect but little from a school (the "unconcerned") are probably screened out quickly. Like the unconcerned, clients who *do* have special needs and interests are no doubt induced, by the exacting affiliation mode, to consider whether extra costs are justified. While involved in this consideration, a client who sees overt signs of special benefits may conclude that extra costs are warranted, and may respond with commitment or, if the school's special emphasis seems unattractive, may decide (as a "dissenter") not to affiliate. A client who sees no signs of school distinctiveness seems likely to conclude that the effort is not worth the candle. By screening out the unconcerned, the dissenters, and those who see nothing special in the school, an exacting affiliation mode presumably could do much to produce a highly committed clientele, homogeneous in terms of educational perceptions and aspirations.

Once the individual has provided the commitment demanded by an exacting affiliation mode, cognitive dissonance and exchange theory suggest that the commitment may require further justification from time to time. In that case, the patron may find additional evidence of school uniqueness (or otherwise reach the conclusion that the costs are warranted and respond with reinforced commitment) or, concluding that the school provides insufficient benefits to justify the costs, may leave. Whether staying or leaving, such a patron contributes further to the homogeneity and commitment of the clientele as a whole (arrow 15). The client's commitment may be enhanced (through a heightened sense of obligation) if the school's special benefits seem at any point to outweigh current contributions.

Some clients, lacking discriminatory powers or the energy and time to use them, may need little or no overt evidence of school uniqueness to support the perception of special school benefits and the commitment that such a perception induces, especially if they are acting under social pressure. Some clients may simply assume, at the point of affiliation, that a school which costs more must be better. Some clients, having decided (for whatever reason) to shoulder the costs which the exacting affiliation mode represents, may justify the costs by convincing themselves (in the absence of evidence, if need be) that the school does, indeed, feature special benefits. They may view the school through rose-colored glasses and respond to what they perceive with enhanced commitment. One would, however, expect the connection between exacting affiliation and client-perceived special mission to be weak when there are no overt indications of school distinctiveness. As was suggested earlier, schools with diffuse, unarticulated, or contradictory goals probably inspire little commitment. Finding no signs of significant school distinctiveness, most clients probably respond apathetically. If the affiliation mode is sufficiently exacting, they probably decide not to affiliate or, if they have already affiliated, decide to disaffiliate. Schools with exacting modes of affiliation may thus be expected to stress and carefully preserve their uniqueness in an effort to survive (arrow 13), while schools with lax modes of affiliation—for example, tax supported schools whose clients perceive that affiliation costs them nothing—should have less need to appear distinctive.

Direct or indirect aid to private schools, when it reaches some level difficult to predict in advance, could not only obliterate the effects of exacting affiliation (depending on whether the private schools responded by reducing their fees), but also produce other serious internal consequences. The prospect should be entertained, in this connection, that only a small proportion of teachers are capable, by virtue of their need dispositions, of responding with intense, enduring commitment to schools approximating the conditions delineated in figure 4 (such as institutional jeopardy, clearly perceived special mission, or exacting client affiliation). If the proportion of people who respond well under such conditions is small, it could turn out that any policies which reduced the exactitude of client affiliation, or in other ways induced a vastly increased inflow of clients to a group of schools, not only would reduce client commitment, as we argued earlier, but also would lead to inferior commitment among the teachers as a whole. Furthermore, public funding could eliminate the need to use the special modes of personnel recruitment, training, assignment, supervision, and remuneration that characterize privately supported schools, and thus could ensure that much potent but latent commitment would never be triggered (arrow 3). Extrinsic motivations, extensively catered to, may displace intrinsic motivations.

Another possible outcome of a more liberal public policy toward the funding of independent schools must be considered: Significant reductions in the exactitude of client affiliation could produce a large shift of student populations from public to private schools, with the consequence that independent schools would become significantly larger in size (see dotted line b immediately above arrow 13). For many reasons I suspect that the interpersonal relationships which distinguish the *Gemeinschaft* school are difficult or even impossible to maintain after schools reach a certain size. Size increases alone could have an enormous debilitating influence on private schools.

A major shift of students from public to private schools could also have the effect, depending on how seriously the founding of new private schools was inhibited by governments, of notably increasing the number of private schools. Insofar as the church-related schools are concerned, it appears that something notable is lost when the existence of a single school closely connected to a church is not enough to accommodate the clamor for student places (this relationship is not directly suggested in figure 4). Such an effect now seems apparent in several Canadian provinces.[22]

I do not mean to suggest, however, that all fiscal relief to private schools, regardless of its form and quantity, is bound to be destructive. The "double taxation" handicap now imposed on private schools is so extreme that they could experience a great deal of economic benefit, whatever its mode, without being enabled to admit patrons without cost, thus abandoning their exacting affiliation practices. In fact, we are now just beginning a study of the effects of provincial support to private schools in British Columbia; though the aid is liberal ($500 per pupil per year) in the context of anything attempted in the United States during the past two decades, the results are far from predictable, especially since the regulatory framework surrounding the aid is as yet rather modest.

Some may wonder why I have engaged in this long discussion concerning the possible subversive, co-optative effects of public money, since significant tax support of private schools seems so unlikely in the United States in the near future, given current Supreme Court guidelines. One reason is that these conditions could eventually change, in which case we should be armed with proper caution. The second reason is more immediate: my analysis suggests strongly, I think, that the nation's public schools would be better off in numerous particulars if government did not continue meeting all their needs from the public coffers. They might be far better equipped to perform as mediating structures if parents had to make some significant direct contributions.

Restrictions on the Freedom of Clients and Educators to Choose or Reject Each Other. There is evidence to suggest that students who affiliate voluntarily with high schools are more committed to several aspects of school life than are students who feel their affiliation was coerced.[23] Parents, also, should evidence higher commitment to schools if they have selected those schools through a process of deliberate choice. The act of

---

[22] *Ibid.*

[23] Richard Nault, "The School Commitments of Nonpublic School Freshmen Voluntarily and Involuntarily Affiliated with Their Schools," in Donald A. Erickson, ed., *Educational Organization and Administration,* Vol. 5 in the American Educational Research Association series, Readings in Educational Research (Berkeley: McCutchan Publishing Corp., 1977), pp. 264–295.

choosing may sensitize parents to school characteristics, otherwise un-noticed, which are gratifying to clients. Having made a choice, human beings do not like to be proved wrong, and hence tend to demonstrate commitment by attempting to ensure that the choice turns out well. The new sense of power conveyed by the freedom to choose schools is impor-tant in its own right, as well as being a source of commitment. The liberty to select schools, if made widely available to parents, could reduce much frustration and conflict by making *flight* an obvious alternative to *fight* whenever parents become angry with educators. Thus, voluntary affilia-tion could defuse conflict and enhance parent and student commitment in all schools, public and independent.

Selective school admissions may have some of the same effects on parent commitment as exacting affiliation is postulated to have (arrows 14 and 27). If, because a school is perceived as highly selective of stu-dents, or it seems difficult to have a child admitted, parents (and stu-dents) may regard affiliation as a scarce, valuable commodity and may respond with enhanced commitment. In addition, selective student admis-sions may contribute significantly to the impression that a school has a special mission (in fact, some independent schools explicitly define their special qualities by referring to their highly selected student bodies), and thus be indirectly conducive to commitment by parents, students, and teachers (arrows 25, 35, 37, 40).

In line with the contentions of numerous other writers, but perhaps more persuasively than any of them, Charles Bidwell argues that many relationships between professionals and clients are based upon trust.[24] Since it is often not feasible for the professional (for example, a physician or attorney) to outline to the client in persuasive detail the complex bodies of logic and evidence that underlie the strategies being undertaken by the professional in behalf of the client, trust is essential. Consequently, Bidwell observes, the professional normally has freedom to reject the client who will not trust, and the client has the same liberty to desert the professional who seems untrustworthy; so clients tend to gravitate to professionals in such a way that the necessary modicum of trust is main-tained in the system. The teaching-learning encounter, as Bidwell sees it, is permeated with the need for trust, yet that trust is often seriously under-mined by the fact that neither party to the engagement may flee or reject the other. Bidwell predicts, then, that the introduction of mutual choice

---

[24] Charles E. Bidwell, "Schooling and Socialization for Moral Commitment," *Inter-change* 3 (1972), pp. 1–27; also see his "Students and Schools: Some Observations on Client-Serving Organizations," in M. R. Rosengren and M. Lefton, eds., *Organiza-tions and Clients: Essays on the Sociology of Service* (Columbus, Ohio: Charles E. Merrill, 1970), pp. 37–70.

into our schooling arrangements will markedly enhance the effectiveness of teaching-learning encounters. If we subsume trust under the concept of student commitment, Bidwell's argument may be considered summarized by arrows 11, 12, 24, and 46.

The relevance of these comments concerning choice becomes evident when one takes note of increasingly frequent contentions in recent years, in both the presence and the absence of proposed fiscal relief for private schools, that families patronizing these schools must not be permitted to segregate themselves along racial, ethnic, socioeconomic, or other lines, and that the schools should not be allowed to produce the same effects through selective student admissions. No doubt these demands are often well intentioned. In the present context it should be obvious, however, that they pose a direct threat to schools as mediating structures. Here, as at virtually every other juncture in educational policy, every benefit involves costs. It is impossible to produce rational decisions on such complex issues unless both sides of the equation are considered.

The same logic applies, of course, to public schools, though within a somewhat different administrative framework of reality. It would be interesting to know how much students and parents have been alienated by the methods generally used to assign youngsters to schools and classrooms.

Some Practical Possibilities

Some steps to rejuvenate, at least partially, the American school as a mediating structure might be briefly mentioned here. I view the recent steps in some public schools systems toward reinvolving parents, more than symbolically, in the education of their offspring as a step in the right direction, for reasons that must now be obvious. I applaud the creation of mini-schools, "alternative schools," and other options within public school systems.

The immediate outlook for measures such as the Moynihan-Packwood tax credit bill to reduce, or even to cease to escalate, the "double taxation" handicap imposed on private schools seems unpromising.

Elsewhere I have discussed at length some temporal and spatial arrangements that could be made to provide more choices and involvement to families.[25] The right, for example, to opt for private rather than public educational offerings may be curtailed, not merely by government-

---

[25] Donald A. Erickson, "The Public-Private Consortium: An Open-Market Model for Educational Reform," in Troy M. McKelvey, ed., *Metropolitan School Organization, Vol. 2: Proposals for Reform* (Berkeley: McCutchan Publishing Corp., 1972), chapter 2.

imposed fiscal handicaps and unduly prescriptive regulations applicable to these offerings, but also by physical and temporal arrangements in public education, enforced under the legal powers of public educational agencies at state, local, and sometimes other levels. It is arguable that many parents who cannot afford to patronize a private school *in toto* in the light of current financial arrangements nevertheless can afford to purchase private educational options made available on a piecemeal (for example, subject-by-subject) basis, and that many parents would do so if given the opportunity. As a specific instance, a parent who is particularly unhappy about the approach of a public school to social studies, but relatively content with the rest of the program, should perhaps be provided with conditions permitting a student to be released from the public school during social studies periods and quickly and easily transferred to premises on which social studies would be offered by some private agency. The same circumstances would make it feasible for groups that cannot sponsor a total school program to develop the discrete components that most interest them.

In light of the strength of organized educators, I am not optimistic in the short haul about breaking public schools and public school systems into human-sized entities once again. In closing, I confess that I find the most hope in despair—that is, I think the current disenchantment of many citizens and lawmakers with the state of education may have to deepen before fundamental change is possible. Even then, the reform may need to be incremental. I find much merit, in this regard, in E. G. West's provocative suggestion that, at some point, we require all future increases in public school funding to be produced through fees collected at the schoolhouse door.[26] If one thinks about that option long enough, and if one considers, in addition, that public education is currently "free" only in a misleading sense, West's method begins to look like the most important single step toward reviving the school as a mediating structure in this modern, complex society.

---

[26] E. G. West, *Nonpublic School Aid* (Lexington, Mass.: Lexington Books, 1976); also his "The Perils of Public Education," *The Freeman* 27 (November 1977), pp. 681–699.

PART TWO

THE CONFERENCE DISCUSSION

Jay Mechling

Finding the Issues

The twenty-one participants in the conference found seats around the "U" of tables in the conference room of Merrill House, a setting appropriate to serious thought about religion and public policy in America. Merrill House is the headquarters of the Council on Religion and International Affairs, the former Church Peace Union founded by Andrew Carnegie. A portrait of the founder hangs on one wall near a facsimile of the charter he wrote when he endowed the organization.

Richard John Neuhaus opened the conference by reviewing purposes and procedures. The phrase "the new shape of the church-state debate" used in preliminary material was not, he said, a declaration of fact so much as expression of a hunch—a hunch that the debate should be recast in significant aspects. Each of four sessions would focus on one of the papers distributed in advance. But at the same time, Neuhaus added, everyone should feel free to relate the discussion to something in the other papers; so that at every point in the conference all papers would legitimately be on the agenda.

Kelley's Points

Neuhaus identified the first speaker, Dean Kelley, as one of the most influential people writing about the church-state question. Kelley's book *Why Churches Should Not Pay Taxes* (Harper & Row, 1977) was well-known to the group. Kelley highlighted three points made in his paper, "Confronting the Danger of the Moment":

First, churches are not just "mediating structures." They have other, and more important functions, from which they may be distracted by the obligations of "mediation." Kelley said the more important function of religion is found in the "meaning enterprise."

Second, the U.S. Supreme Court continues to strike down state tax credit programs for parents who send their children to private or parochial schools. While raising questions about the correctness of the Court's view, Kelley saw no reason to expect a more positive ruling on tax credit proposals, including the Moynihan-Packwood bill, then before Congress.

Third, Kelley outlined his difficulties with "subsidiarity," an issue that framed much of the discussion on the first day. His opposition to churches and their schools taking subsidies from government is based on the dictum, "The queen's shilling will sooner or later be followed by the queen." When it comes to the possibility of control and co-optation, the difference between a private contributor's money and public funds is that the former does not "bear the force of law," Kelley said. He claimed that attempts are already underway to define religion in increasingly restrictive terms, seemingly to try to get the church back into the sanctuary and keep it there. As evidence, he cited *Ohio* v. *Whisner,* involving state efforts to regulate parochial schools; *McClure* v. *Salvation Army,* an attempt to apply federal equal employment regulations to religious institutions; and moves by the National Labor Relations Board to regulate hiring and firing practices in parochial schools.

Kelley's paper developed a thesis linking recent church-state legal cases with the notion of mediating structures Berger and Neuhaus presented in *To Empower People* which proposes consideration of public support for the social and educational agencies of churches as mediating structures. Kelley was skeptical of this proposal. The pivotal issue, he said, is whether church-related schools and social service agencies will be able to rely upon public money without having to worry about how they will be affected as mediating structures. What good does it do private institutions to be private, Kelley asked, if they become more and more indistinguishable from the public institutions?

Reflecting a separationist position, Kelley's proposed "extraterritoriality" as a public policy allowing the church to function as a mediating structure without becoming controlled by government. Churches and other mediating structures, he insisted, must be exempt from the controls the Internal Revenue Service, the National Labor Relations Board, and other government agencies exert on business. But he argued that this constitutionally warranted separation need not keep mediating structures out of the public forum. Kelley vigorously defended the right of churches to speak out on political matters related to the public interest. In making this point, he departed from his paper to comment on the Tenth Circuit Court of Appeals' decision in *Christian Echoes National Ministry, Inc.* v. *U.S.,* the 1972 ruling involving the work of an anti-Communist fundamentalist preacher, Billy James Hargis. Kelley said:

> Congress, apparently troubled by an excess of democratic practice, introduced into the Internal Revenue Code a clause, in Section 501(c)(3), that no exempt (deductible) organization shall engage to any "substantial" degree in attempts to in-

fluence legislation. This was such a successful ploy that a few years later Senator Lyndon B. Johnson introduced an additional clause, that neither should exempt organizations engage at all—not even to an insubstantial degree—in attempts to influence an election.

The upshot of those clauses, at least as interpreted by the Tenth Circuit Court in *Chistian Echoes,* is that any organization exempt under Section 501(c)(3) obtain its exemption at the price of relinquishing its right to engage in civil discourse, if that discourse has any impact, in any way, upon present or prospective legislation.

That really is one of the biggest blots upon religious liberties in this country today. The Tenth Circuit announced, in so many words, that Billy James Hargis did not lose any of his religious liberties as a result of being deprived of his tax exemption for engaging in attempts to influence legislation. He was still free to do that, without his exemption. But if he wanted tax exemption, he'd have to quit. Now what is that but requiring a person, in order to enjoy tax exemption, to abandon rights guaranteed by the Constitution?

Kelley ended his remarks by warning against a vision of society "so completely and successfully imbued with mediating structures that they form each sectarian pillar" as in the Netherlands. That "horror" story, Kelley added, is not the present danger in the United States but should be considered as a possible extreme to be avoided.

Individual Position Speeches

Peter Berger, who chaired the discussion of Dean Kelley's paper, offered one initial observation: Kelley disagreed with the "maximalist" position on mediating structures but agreed with the "minimalist" view that encourages them by leaving them alone. Berger then opened the issue to general discussion. What followed was a series of short, individual position speeches on mediating structures in general and the school issue, vis-à-vis church-state relations, in particular.

Arthur Hertzberg introduced an especially relevant theme, namely, the attitude of religious-cultural minorities toward mediating structures in a society in which all structures tend to mediate in favor of the majority culture. He addressed himself to the Jewish experience in America, noting, of course, its diversities. Ultra-Orthodox Jews, Hertzberg said, always live in "exile" so the nature of the *goyim* among whom they live is irrelevant to them. Since they are "waiting for the Messiah," the Ultra-Orthodox are interested not in integrating with a larger society, but in survival. Therefore, they find it proper to take from the outside society whatever helps them survive. The broader culture is "the other," not necessarily the enemy, though it might be.

> In the mainstream of the Jewish community, experience with mediating structures is a profound, historical affair, and that is why I asked for the floor very early, in order to add these premises to the discussion. Jewish historical experience, to the degree to which Jews want to integrate into society, is anti-mediating structures. That is the fundamental proposition. Jewish historical experience regards mediating structures as the enemy, regards the existence of mediating structures as the possibility of attack. Why?

Hertzberg cited historical examples—notably from eighteenth century Europe—that provide grounds for debate on mediating structures within the Jewish community. But his point was that as Jews moved toward emancipation in the nineteenth century, they moved against mediating structures because those structures were oppressive; the mediating structures of others—chiefly the church—were the symbols of what was oppressive. Hertzberg continued:

> Therefore, oddly enough, the Jewish community, that is supposed to be the most historically minded of all communities, is, in the last few centuries, the most antihistory. You cannot understand modern Jewish experience unless you understand that it exists to dynamite—to *dynamite*—the society that existed before the emancipation. And that dynamiting is directed mainly toward mediating structures or, at the very least, their privatization; therefore, the passion of Jews for the separation of church and state. It is an old, historic sore. And, by the way, it recurs. Read Hannah Arendt's historiography on the Holocaust.[1] It is about the fact that there still existed (in Nazi Europe) a Jewish mediating structure, the Jewish leadership of the ghetto, and better that it had not been. There would have been no structure with which to find Jews and to oppress them, and to send them off to Auschwitz. . . .
>
> When you talk to me about mediating structures, what you arose from me is . . . let me read you a couple of the nastier notes in front of me: 'If I had Dean Kelley's Valhalla, where the mediating structures were entirely free of government regulation and left alone, where the oppressive weight of this impersonal government were not upon them, how would I stop schools like Gerald L. K. Smith's from teaching anti-Semitism?'. . .

---

[1] Hannah Arendt, *The Origins of Totalitarianism* (New York: Harcourt, Brace & Company, 1950).

"I beg your pardon?" Dean Kelley said.

Hertzberg reformulated his point: "How does one in your heaven get inside that school and make sure that it does not preach anti-Semitism?"

"How does one get inside a public school in New York City?" Donald Erickson wondered.

"Exactly," replied Hertzberg. "I'm getting to that. The problems that Jews have with mediating structures are rather deeper than other traditions, and the problems Jews have with democratic governments are rather less. Because democratic governments at their 'most oppressive' and 'most totalitarian' are still more manageable than are mediating structures left totally loose."

Hertzberg returned to the public school issue, insisting that the essential problem is that the white middle class (including Jews) has abandoned the public school to the poor, so that the people who are proposing public support of private education are those who no longer have children in public schools. He asked why we must presume it is unfair for the middle class, and beyond, to be taxed in a variety of ways for the maintenance of center city as a dumping ground for the poor. Why not find it reasonable for the middle class to bear the double burden of supporting both public and private schools?

David Seeley, acknowledging that the separation doctrine is a pragmatic solution for peace in a pluralistic society, inquired whether we have gone too far in the direction of a *Gesellschaft* society. Perhaps the challenge of this conference, Seeley speculated, was to reformulate the *Gemeinschaft/Gesellschaft* balance as it must be sought in the next few decades.

Berger offered a succinct summary of Hertzberg's concerns: "Is modernity good for the Jews?"

Milton Himmelfarb said that the rise of powerful government in the twentieth century and the rise of a new class whose power depends upon an expansion of government services and bureaucracy have rendered classical Jewish resistance to mediating structures "anachronistic." He admitted increasing inclination toward libertarian individualism despite communitarian tendencies.

Government having been repeatedly branded as an unchecked power, Donald Erickson added another social culprit: professionalization, which has wrested control of the public schools from the lay public. Erickson said parents feel more power when they have their children in private schools, which tend to be less under the control of professionals. John Coleman agreed that professional monopoly is as much the enemy today as is government. He gave an example of a Roman Catholic hospital that successfully resisted federal control only to cave in to the medical profession.

At this point, James Wood reaffirmed the strict separationist position taken in Kelley's paper. Baptists, he reminded the group, oppose attempts to use public funds for private schools. Wood said he was bothered by talk of "pragmatic" reasons for the First Amendment; to view such an important principle as pragmatic does disservice both to its eighteenth century context and to the present relationship between government and organized religion.

Joseph Sullivan questioned the underlying ecclesiology in some of the participants' use of the term "church." Based on his experience in working with the poor in New York City, Sullivan said he was convinced that viable mediating structures, such as the church, must deal with the lives of the poor at the street level. He acknowledged a threat to the churches from government meddling, such as the Internal Revenue ruling that churches cannot poll political candidates and publicize their views, and to mediating structures from unions and professions, but he maintained that mediating structures cannot serve the poor if they are isolated from government. To help the people who have no alternative to the public school system, he said, a mediating structure can try to effect change only by working in some way with government—by taking some government money while maintaining some credibility with its constituency because it is knowledgeable about what is going on. In the split between the strict separationists and those willing to accept the queen's shilling while resisting control, Sullivan favored a symbiotic relationship with government.

Peter Berger pointed out a major disagreement: there was obviously no consensus on receiving subsidization, while at the same time resisting regulation, an issue that was "the absolute heart problem of this conference."

Richard Morgan, speaking to Kelley, said that American constitutional history was rich with examples in which the queen did not follow the queen's shilling. "The queen," he said, "sends her regulatory means where the subtle, intellectual, political consensus of the period dictates," but there is nothing constitutionally necessary in the relationship between subsidy and control. Further, Morgan was troubled by Kelley's conclusions on "extraterritoriality." As a person who works for a mediating structure (Bowdoin College) that is not church-related, Morgan wanted the churches as allies in the struggle against unwise and overobtrusive government regulation. To him, Kelley's concept of extraterritoriality suggested a picture of the churches "drawing the constitutional mantle around them and withdrawing from the field."

Kelley and Morgan sparred on the question, "Does regulation have a constitutional warrant?" Kelley argued that Justice Robert Jackson's dictum—on the authority of government to regulate that which it subsidizes—would prevail, and he challenged Morgan to cite cases in which the constitutional case went against control. Morgan's example was higher education, but he emphasized a more general point, the difference between "must regulate" and "may regulate." The latter is subject to political struggle, which can be turned around.

Kelley agreed, saying that it is "may regulate" which the courts have established and is now subject to political pressure.

Morgan cited Ward Elliott's study of the Supreme Court reapportionment decisions which reflected a consensus developed in American society from the 1930s to the 1960s[2]. Those interested in the health of mediating structures should aim their fire not at the Court or the bureaucrats, Morgan said, but at the academics, the writers, and other intellectuals. Out of their experience with the Depression and the civil rights movement, they created a consensus about the role of government in the institutions of the private sector, which Morgan thought was "fundamentally mistaken."

Arthur Hertzberg detected in this conversation an antigovernment, antibureaucracy drift he wanted to resist. To him, the New Deal bureaucracy was a social escalator for Jews and other minorities, just as the present federal bureaucracy is the prime creator of the black middle class. This social mobility has created its share of anomie and destroyed senses of community, but Hertzberg was not sure that the old communities were always good. He returned to the issues of suburban versus inner-city schools and again insisted that the real problem is the social class character of schools.

Richard Neuhaus found in Hertzberg's remarks an occasion to clarify the idea of "empowerment" as expressed in the mediating structures project. Hertzberg might see federal bureaucracy as benign, but what of Jesse Jackson's critique of the pattern of dependency created by government paternalism in the public schools and elsewhere? To "empower" the poor, Neuhaus said, means to provide the poor with the public funds to decide for themselves what sort of education they want for their children—to go to private schools if they wish.

Hertzberg wanted to summarize his argument: on balance, he was more trusting of a government "under scrutiny" than of the substructures that are mediating structures. As a member of a minority, he felt he had access to and control over government to a degree not true for substructures. He would take the difficulties of big government over the diffi-

---

[2] Ward Elliott, *The Rise of Guardian Democracy: The Supreme Court's Role in Rights Disputes 1848–1969* (Cambridge: Harvard University Press, 1974).

culties raised by substructures with radically increased power, because the latter would mean a series of enclaves hampering social unity.

At Berger's request, Dean Kelley agreed to open the next session with a list of key issues explored that morning.

Four Issues

Dean Kelley enumerated four issues which he thought had emerged from the preceding discussion. Before listing them, he recounted that the National Council of Churches had recently departed from its previous policy in accepting three federal government grants—one for work with incarcerated veterans, another for energy education, and a third for a VISTA volunteer education program; Kelley, who had unsuccessfully opposed all three, pointed out that the organization faced precisely the issues raised in the discussion following his paper. The issues he set forth were:

• The question of the queen's shilling, or the relationship between subsidy and control. What barriers can be defended, and are the barriers permeable in only one direction, that is, can churches participate in politics but expect freedom from government regulation?

• Professionalization and its potential threat to mediating structures, even in the absence of governmental control.

• The question whether trust should be put in government or in mediating structures.

• The meaning of individual freedom in the context of community rights.

On the fourth issue, Kelley drew attention to the view of the backyards of the brownstones along 64th Street, in New York City. From the balcony of the second floor conference room, each beautiful green garden looked like a haven from the city, and each one was walled impenetrably from the others. Was this walled world a metaphor for the segmented society to come, Kelley wondered.

Berger remarked that one of the issues of the conference concerned the definition of the "wall" between church and state. Another "wall" issue was how big are the barriers to be around the Balkanizing communities in American society. How do the two wall issues relate?

Frank Butler wanted to add one more consideration to the discussion. Public policy, he said, almost always involves moral issues. How, in a situation of cultural pluralism, can public policy benefit from the moral content, and the moral wisdom, that resides in mediating structures?

Richard Neuhaus wanted to refine that question further. He wondered whether a "folk church," one involved with the lives of the poor on a day-to-day basis, can play a prophetic role in supplying moral wisdom to public policy, in contributing to the formation of a moral consensus? Berger asked why a folk church would have any more difficulty than another church in playing a prophetic role, and Neuhaus replied that Dean Kelley and James Wood shared the view that the church can be prophetic only if it hermetically seals itself off from any dependence upon the queen's shilling. Joseph Sullivan's view, however, was that it was necessary to play the game with the government to be effective. "I'm sure they all would say that they want to be prophetic, but with a different understanding of the contribution of the mediating structures to the formation of public policy," Neuhaus concluded.

To talk of the "prophetic" role of the church standing outside of society is to talk like a Protestant, said Arthur Hertzberg. This is an ethnic and class-oriented view that overlooks the fact that biblical religion allows for a prophetic role *within* government, according to the Jewish leader.

James Wood introduced the matter of accountability into the discussion, and Hertzberg turned to that. America, he said, is rapidly moving toward Balkanization, and regional and ethnic consciousness are its symptoms. He was concerned that certain ethnic mediating structures are becoming less and less accountable to the larger society, for example, hospitals in New York City becoming more ethnic and being defended as ethnic preserves, or unions controlling other mediating structures. These are the successors to Tammany Hall—"sacred cows running amuck in the name of ethnicity," said Hertzberg.

The fault, according to Joseph Sullivan, is that the government "bought" these substructures, these mediating structures, as the means for effecting change, but it bought them for the wrong reasons. Accountability has been not to public purpose but to process, with no agreement on the desirability or product or process. Mediating structures will not take over all social services, Sullivan insisted, but they will affect how all services are defined and delivered. He found this the greatest impact mediating structures can have upon government subsidized services.

Neuhaus wanted to clarify the understanding of accountability he and Berger presented in *To Empower People*—"that community services in their definition and structure and delivery should be accountable to the people who are the consumers." This is not a case for decentralization, which could be more totalitarian than the present arrangement. In the ensuing discussion, the topics of accountability and professionalization became intermingled in a way that did not clarify the relation between the two.

Christa Klein discussed her research on American Protestant seminary education and the effect of professionalization on the delivery of services by elites. Her work has shown that seminarians are faced with the dilemma of professional and governmental expectations in conflict with their religious faith.

Richard Morgan posed the question: What are the limits of the tolerable with regard to mediating structures? Are we willing to tolerate their eccentricities?

Berger tried to sort out three kinds of accountability, calling them "worries." First is the worry about "religio-ethnic gangsterism." Second is the worry that some totalitarian bureaucrat will destroy the churches. Third is the worry that there is voluntary kowtowing to so-called experts and professionals.

This catalog of worries struck a chord in Dean Kelley, who offered some examples of responses by groups to such worries. The "accountability" of lobbies is the banner under which Congress is working on a bill to regulate lobbying activities of tax-exempt mediating structures, and the same cry for accountability is behind moves to open all meetings of the National Council of Churches to the press. The real accountability of a voluntary organization, Kelley said emphatically, is to its members, not to the public in general. Of course, he added, this case is much harder to make if the voluntary association accepts public funds.

John Coleman's Summary

John Coleman prefaced his summary of his paper with observations on the recent history of the church-state debate. He called attention to the fact that the literature on the theological issues of the debate stops in the 1960s, because the debate fractured into three parts: (1) the debate over "civil religion," in which the place of theological argument is uncertain; (2) the debate over civil disobedience, in which the relevant issue is the limits of obedience to the state; and (3) the debate over liberation theology and the role of the church in public policy.

Coleman said his paper dealt only with the third direction the debate has taken, and he cited Richard Neuhaus's *Christian Faith and Public Policy* (1977) as a good example of this debate. One question here, he noted, is "What kind of understanding of the First Amendment is fair to the freedom of the church?"

Coleman recalled a portion of the morning's discussion which seemed to him to misinterpret John Courtney Murray's view of the First Amendment. The First Amendment is based not upon a pragmatic arrangement, he said, but upon "a very high moral idea of the self-denying state." The Founding Fathers, said Coleman, envisioned not a Hegelian state but an organic, Christian society.

92

Clearly evident in Coleman's paper was the author's belief—not without its dilemmas, he admitted—that every theological position relates to a sociological position, and vice versa. Policy issues could be shown to flow from all sets of church-state doctrines, but rather than devote his paper to such a Herculean task, Coleman chose to do for his particularist position (Roman Catholic) what he would like to do for all—"to show where, at certain crucial points, the theology subsumes a social philosophy." Every theology, he said, owes it to its members and to the public to lay out its public policy implications.

Coleman drew attention to his distinction between "public theology," that is, the public policy implications of a particular identity system stated explicitly for everyone, and "civil discourse," or "secular warrant." If civil discourse is to take place, he said, at some point people must be able to deal with public policy issues not immediately tied to their own particularist theological symbol system.

Two questions were on Coleman's mind: the dangers involved in accepting the queen's shilling, and the matter of power corrupting. The clear message of the previous discussion, Coleman said, was that the queen's shilling represents an extreme danger for the church. Dean Kelley's ecclesiology warned of this danger, and Donald Erickson's paper would provide examples of schools whose power as alternative mediating structures were undermined by subsidy. Coleman saw this as a problem for the church but not as a church-state problem, not a problem the church need adjudicate. He noted that William Ball's paper would indicate the supineness, the lack of courage, shown by church people in the face of pressure or temptation from the state. If the church "sells out," he warned, then we shall lose our pluralism. In the example cited of the Catholic hospital in Baltimore, Coleman said we should not blame the state for exacting regulations in exchange for the queen's shilling; we should blame the sisters who run the hospital and the professional monopoly that controls definitions of health care.

On the corrupting nature of power, Coleman tendered the possibility that mediating structures may not always be the source of liberation. Society is, he said, in a new moment in the history of mediating structures, and must assess the "danger of the moment." The danger of power corrupting is not, however, always assessed in the same way, as was exemplified by the different responses to the so-called Bundy money made available for higher education by the state of New York. Fordham University, historically Catholic and now listed as "independent," took the position that accepting state funds would not undermine its mission as a religious institution. Le Moyne College, a Catholic institution in Syracuse, refused the money.

93

Faith Rights and Public Rights

James Wood said Coleman's use of Thomas Sanders's work was a distortion of the separationist position. A recitation on Baptist ideology and a brief exchange of views on history ensued. Peter Berger returned the conversation to the point Coleman had made about the queen's shilling being a church problem, not a church-state problem. "Dean Kelley could not have written his paper if he had not been a Christian," Berger said. "I think Richard Neuhaus and I could have written *To Empower People* if we were not Christians, or religious in any sense. There are different worries involved. The central worry in Dean's paper is a worry about the religious community. The central worry in *To Empower People* is about American society." If Kelley were right about the dangers, Berger wondered, might we ask the church to undergo them for the welfare of society?

Kelley responded quickly. Separation of church and state is a constitutional ideal, he said. The individual has rights in the civil city irrespective of his or her religious affiliation, and one need not go through the church in order to secure one's rights as an individual. The church and state have very different functions that should not be mixed; church and state should not try to imitate one another.

"Would you want churches to take this position, even if you were not a Christian?" Neuhaus asked.

Kelley replied that he would because he felt that it is not meritorious for the church or any mediating structure to "sacrifice" itself for the state. To do so would be to lose the mediating function, and that would be a serious loss.

David Seeley addressed a question about education to John Coleman. Concluding that public education is not neutral but rather an "engine of modernization," Seeley asked whether the churches, which have a Christian society as their goal, should not worry about this secular "engine." That is exactly the worry religious people have, Coleman responded. Religious people know that secular institutions do establish a religious position. Coleman and Seeley agreed that churches should urge the public schools to recognize the religious nature of public schooling.

James Rudin brought the conversation back to Berger's concern whether society might ask churches to take a risk for the sake of social welfare. He wondered whether the proposition really asked the churches to sacrifice themselves to big government. In sketching the real world context in which risk, mediation, and religious expression take place, Rudin shared some personal history. He was raised in a part of Virginia where the only Jewish mediating structures were his home and the synagogue. His public school and boys' club were predominantly Baptist; his

Boy Scout troop met in the First Baptist Church. The public mediating structures with which he grew up were predominantly Southern Baptist.

The conversation was moving toward a focused issue, put by Richard Neuhaus: "At what point do the faith rights that we claim impinge upon or come into conflict with the legitimate rights of the community?"

The course to that issue began with Rudin's recollections on growing up Jewish in a Southern Baptist context and moved through Peter Berger's elucidation of the battle of Protestant evangelical schools against state regulation in North Carolina. Berger said he was sure these schools from his point of view, teach all kinds of reprehensible things. "But I feel these people are fighting my battle, and I am totally on their side against the state of North Carolina." As a sociologist, Berger was sure these evangelicals were correct—the public schools of North Carolina and the regulations the state would impose upon them are detrimental to their faith.

Berger laid out three levels of policy to consider in relation to the evangelical schools: (1) the evangelicals insist upon absolute freedom to run their schools; (2) they expect tax credits for parents of pupils in the schools; and (3) they expect public subsidies. Dean Kelley would support one and two but would be very nervous about three, Berger pointed out, asking where others in the group stood on this concrete case.

James Wood protested the distinction between policies two and three, a distinction Kelley would accept. Everyone appeared to find the first policy—leaving the evangelicals to run their own schools—perfectly reasonable, until James Rudin asked if we could be comfortable giving schools total freedom if they were teaching anti-black doctrines.

Albert Huegli pointed out precedents in education and elsewhere for government to issue regulations meant to protect "the welfare of the whole community." There are some things, he said, that people are entitled to as citizens of a community, and there are some things that the community is entitled to expect from people, for the benefit of the whole community. That is where the discussion must begin, he concluded, in terms of making public policy decisions that balance individual and community rights.

James Wood repeated his argument that accepting tax credits and accepting outright subsidies amounts to the same thing: in both cases the school accepting preferential treatment would forfeit its right to claim exemption from governmental controls and standards. The government challenge to the tax exemption of Bob Jones University, the South Carolina institution accused of racist admissions policy, provided an example.

Dean Kelley said the Bob Jones University case was based upon the erroneous assumption that exemption is a status conferred by the grace of government, a status that can be given or taken away. Kelley's book

Why Churches Should Not Pay Taxes argues against this assumption; churches do not produce "wealth" as we understand it, so the churches should not be taxed on that basis. Kelley moved on to draw distinctions between "tax exemptions," "tax credits," and "deductible contributions." Wood insisted again that tax credits are reimbursements.

Neuhaus observed that racism seemed to be the nagging issue in regard to the accountability of mediating structures. Both he and Berger, he said, were sensitive to the criticism that *To Empower People* was arbitrary in singling out racism as the one element of pluralism not to be tolerated. While there are historical and political arguments to support special safeguards against racism, Neuhaus admitted that he and Berger had no entirely satisfactory answer to their critics.

The discussion returned to the example of evangelical schools in North Carolina. Richard Morgan took the view that these schools should be allowed to teach whatever they like so long as they meet the state's minimal accreditation standards.

What if an ideology lurks in the accreditation standards, Neuhaus responded. Donald Erickson asked where the line should be drawn between freedom of the press, or freedom of speech in general, and comparable freedom in schools. When we move from society to the schools, why should we lose that freedom?

Several comments contrasted the teaching of skills and the teaching of values in schools. Erickson stressed the jeopardy of private schools at present—jeopardy arising in part from resistance to the formation of fundamentalist (sometimes "oddball") schools, which threaten state education establishments. He said that in Kentucky, North Carolina, and elsewhere educational establishments are launching virulent attacks upon the new schools.

Erickson asked how church agencies might be persuaded to take a more principled stand on regulation. He offered the example of an ongoing dispute in Kentucky, where the state has tried to make an evangelical school meet state regulations. Leaders of some Catholic schools, he said, will accept state regulations in exchange for public funds because they think they have the political power to resist further regulations after they get the money.

> What is happening, ladies and gentlemen, is that the freedom of a lot of oddball, little schools that want to be different from public education, and want to experiment with something that may be important, are being undermined by some of our religious leaders who are adopting a very opportunistic, unprincipled stand on this question of state regulations.

Joseph Sullivan defended the right of the state, under the "public health and safety" principle, to decide that a school cannot teach "antianything," especially "anti-any person" in society. Neuhaus asked Sullivan how one drew the line between tolerable and intolerable doctrines taught in a school. How is the line drawn between racism and other freedoms of speech?

Sullivan replied that racism is the source of a profound dualism that is destructive and unacceptable. Schools are quite different from newspapers; schools deal with young minds, so the freedom of speech cannot be interpreted in the same way. Society has the right to protect itself against the sort of education that tends to divide it, he stated. John Coleman agreed, saying that the state enjoyed the right to intervene in *every* school, public or private, to protect its legitimate concerns.

We might ask if the churches have the nerve to organize against injustice, Sullivan said, but Erickson objected, asking, who has the wisdom to make decisions about what may or may not be taught in school. To protect children from indoctrination we would have to censor books, television, movies, and the like.

James Dunn took Erickson's worry as a warrant for the strict separationist view he shared with James Wood.

While persuaded by Erickson of the lack of empirical evidence that schools affect children's values, Berger worried that this view could be pushed far enough to abolish any legal recognition of the concept of childhood. Berger also voiced strong reservations about the "children's rights movement." There is such a thing as childhood, and children are more vulnerable to influence.

John Coleman warned that the conversation seemed to lack a clear definition of "mediating structures." Without an idea of what constitutes a mediating structure and how it generates distinctive values and "community," we might not move beyond general propositions, he said. Perhaps, said Christa Klein, mediating structures cannot be discussed in the singular. Perhaps reference should be to clusters of mediating structures. For example, James Rudin's autobiographical anecdotes showed that the Baptist schools and Boy Scouts were not as important to him as were his family and synagogue. People might be better off for all the friction between competing mediating structures, she suggested.

I stepped out of my role as *rapporteur* at this point to observe that the tendency of the discussion had been to view children as victims, but

> the evidence is that children are a good deal more resilient than we adults give them credit for being. In fact, almost all children play, and one of the things they learn in play is role-distance. I don't want us to discount the ability of children to resist that which they are not naturally prone to believe anyway. And I don't want to discount the ability of children to have within their own "folk culture" support for resistance to adult culture.

Perhaps the power of schools, Coleman said, lies in the way they can empower children with the values of their family and ethnic group.

Neuhaus offered a quick concluding comment. "In planning this conference we thought that today's sessions would focus on the more general church-state questions, and yet we have done exactly what most discussions of the issue end up doing. We have focused ourselves very much on education—and on James Rudin's education!" He expressed the hope that in the next day's discussion, in which schools would be prominent, some of the larger issues—such as the distinction between state and society, or the ways in which mediating structures shape the ethos and value systems by which public policy is formed—would come up as well.

As the participants dispersed, I tried to formulate in my mind what exactly the day had accomplished. The accomplishment, I decided, was that issues and networks of alliances became public.

Exploring the Issues

Peter Berger introduced William B. Ball, the Harrisburg attorney prominent in some of the cases that had been mentioned or discussed at the conference. Ball spoke about two issues of deep concern to him. First, he summarized the events and court cases that led to the present status of Supreme Court decisions on church-state matters in education. Second, he addressed the threats he saw to the freedom of private, especially religious, educational institutions. Another way to state this second concern, Ball said, was to call it the issue of the freedom of parents to choose the education they want for their children.

The Supreme Court's present interpretation of the application of the First Amendment to private and religious schools, Ball began, is really the culmination of a series of accidents. In the early 1960s, the Court looked at Pennsylvania and Maryland school prayer regulations and, in the Schempp opinion, laid down a test of what the establishment clause meant. The Schempp decision included the "purpose and effect" test: (1) Does the legislation or program have a secular purpose? (2) Does the legislation or program have the purpose of advancing or prohibiting religion? This test was applied to the textbook loan program in New York, for example, and in *Board of Education* v. *Allen* the Court upheld that program based on a "dual function" concept, that is, that the religious (Catholic) schools using the textbooks served both secular and religious purposes.

In *Lemon* v. *Kurzman* the Court went far beyond the "purpose and effect" rule when it struck down a Pennsylvania program of purchasing from religious organizations certain welfare services for children, including the teaching of "nonreligious" subjects such as math, modern languages, physical education, and science. That decision spoke of the "excessive entanglement" of church and state—leading to an establishment of religion—when the state attempted to guarantee that, say, math would not be taught in a religious atmosphere.

The "ever ingenious" Pennsylvania legislature, Ball continued, then enacted a tuition grant program it thought would not be entangling and would not lead to the establishment of religion. This program gave partial reimbursements to parents who sent their children to religious schools, but the reimbursements were not earmarked for any specific use. Parents could use the money for any purpose. The Supreme Court struck down this program in *Lemon* v. *Sloan,* arguing that the effect of the program was the establishment of religion because the primary beneficiaries would be members of one religion, Roman Catholicism. Similarly, the Court has struck down state programs that supported public teachers of auxiliary services (such as speech and hearing or remedial reading) in private schools.

Programs in any of these forms appear to be held unconstitutional by the Supreme Court, Ball said. On the present Court, he counted at least six votes against any substantial aid to religious schools. The attorney speculated that the Moynihan-Packwood tax credit proposals would be able to get by the Court only if the justices accept a theory they have not previously endorsed, namely, "that it is the responsibility of the public to accommodate religious and parental freedom, that the free exercise and personal liberty considerations should outweigh establishment clause considerations."

In an observation touching on the previous day's discussion of "accountability," Ball said that he was deeply troubled by the requirement of the tax credit legislation before Congress that the credit be given only if the child attends a school "accredited or approved" by the state education authority. Ball said this requirement has great dangers and that he would prefer to see the credit given if the school comports with the compulsory attendance law. "The 'accredited or approved' wording seems to me to be an open invitation to the state education departments to set up accreditation and approval machinery which will amount to the licensing of all private education."

His comments on the Moynihan-Packwood bill led to his second area of concern—threats to private education. This was the issue claiming the most attention in his paper. The fundamental question here, Ball said, was "whether people may form natural groupings, for religious or educational reasons, create schools, pay for them themselves, do it because of impulsion of conscience, and be relatively let alone by the state." Such was the question in *Ohio* v. *Whisner,* a case in which Ball participated two years earlier. That case involved parents, who had their children in their own Tabernacle Christian School, indicted by a grand jury on charges of truancy. Their school did not meet the minimum state standards to qualify legally as a school. The Ohio standards, it was revealed during the case, number over 600 and constitute a 126 page book. Were these standards laws or recommendations? Some of the standards violated the religious principles of Tabernacle Christian School, some were financially impossible (such as a requirement that schools have multimedia labs), and others were simply incomprehensible, Ball reported. The parents won that case, but similar cases are still pending. Ball explained that in such litigation the legal burden of the state is to show a "compelling state interest" in limiting what must be a valid religious liberty claimed by the defense.

Before the floor was opened for discussion, Ball also reviewed attempts of the National Labor Relations Board, the Department of Commerce, the Internal Revenue Service, and the Secretary of Labor to control churches and church schools as though they were businesses.

Anticipating the Court

Several persons asked Ball, one of the nation's most informed authorities on church-state issues in the courts, to speculate on pending issues. Albert Huegli asked if the voucher system was a form of aid that would be outlawed by the courts. A voucher program, Ball responded, could be struck down under the *Lemon* v. *Sloan* decision, which ruled against Pennsylvania's plan to reimburse parents of students in private schools. A voucher creates a direct link between the state and the school—a link Ball believed would be interpreted as violating the no establishment clause. Is that also true of the tax credit plan for the parents of college students, Huegli asked. No, Ball said, the courts have found church-related colleges to be "not all that religious," and Ball also thought the courts would accept the argument that, if the government could make outright grants and loans to church-related colleges, then it could also extend some tax credits to the parents of persons attending those colleges.

David Seeley asked if there might be hope that the Supreme Court would develop two related doctrines. First, would the Court base a decision not upon the question of religious liberty but upon the rights of parents to have their values protected? Second, is there any truth in a rumor that the Court is willing to state a doctrine of the "least burdensome" implementation of a court action if a court finds compelling state interest to limit religious or personal liberty? In short, Seeley asked Ball to comment upon the legal aspects of the earlier discussion of the relationship between parents' rights and the public interest.

In reply to the second question, Ball insisted that there are alternative means for private schools to demonstrate that the legitimate, compelling interests of the state are being met in their schools. These are not the interests of the educational bureaucracy, but the legitimate interests of the public in having a people who can read, write, and do math. Private schools could point to achievement test scores to prove the state's interests have been met. But states seem reluctant to accept this evidence, probably because the public schools would be unable to withstand this same scrutiny. That remark brought peals of laughter.

But are the courts, pressed Seeley, likely to accept the "least burdensome" approach in protecting the state's interests? The courts have never done this, said Ball. They came closest in *Wisconsin* v. *Yoder,* the Amish case. The Supreme Court decided that the Amish are providing an alternative means of education through their home study procedure, which is another way of saying it met the state's legitimate interests.

In response to Seeley's first question, about the protection of parents' values, the only case that came to Ball's mind was *Farrington* v. *Tokushige,* in the 1930s, in which the Court determined it was invalid for the state to try to prescribe all that happens in a private school.

> Parents should get tax credits for sending their children to private schools not on the theory that the schools aren't religious but on the theory that they are religious. The fact that a child is enrolled in such a school and the government helps his parents means that the government is accommodating a thing that is in the public interest, namely, religious liberty. Any tension we have between the "free exercise" and "establishment" concepts ought to be resolved in favor of "free exercise," in my opinion.

James Dunn raised an issue that others also identified as a problem. Without state minimal standards for schools, what can be done to control those who prey upon frightened church schools in order to distribute perhaps educationally inadequate materials to them? What, he further wondered, could be done to stop frauds and profiteering in educational materials? Ball replied that fraud laws already prohibit racketeering; moreover, parents know what is good education for their children, and the judgments of parents should be trusted.

The Court and Religious Liberty

Given Ball's pessimism about the present Supreme Court on tax credits or other aid to private education, Richard Neuhaus wondered if the Court would continue to move toward a narrower definition of the role of religion in society. Ball's response was somewhat surprising. He said he thought there was in past Court decisions the foundation upon which to build a sound religious liberty doctrine. The "entanglement" concept, for example, was sound, if not well-applied in *Lemon* v. *Kurzman.* Justice Black acknowledged in that decision the tension between the free exercise clause and the establishment clause. And in a recent religious liberty case—involving a Tennessee clergyman—Justice Brennan wrote in a concurring majority opinion a good essay on religious liberty and the right of religious bodies to go into the public forum to advocate. This decision wisely overthrows the idea that the establishment clause was meant to avoid political divisions along religious lines.

"One of the toughest things in religious liberty litigation," Ball confided, "is to get judges to understand at some rudimentary level what 'religious' is." Some judges seem unable to distinguish between specific sets of doctrines and faith communities. Ball's view was that any interference with a faith community is an interference with religious liberty, that attacks upon religious liberty are not always and clearly attacks upon religious doctrine.

Berger inquired into the origins of the principles the Court has used in striking down private school aid programs. Do the decisions represent some sort of judicial logic working in a social vacuum? Or are they the result of a secularization process? Berger suggested the latter.

"Whether or not the Supreme Court is an active force in the secularizing process is a very complex question," replied Ball, who thought it entirely appropriate that we have secular public schools and found no problems with the Court's decisions on public school Bible reading and prayer. He would be troubled, however, by a decision upholding the National Labor Relations Board in its attempts to force religious schools to abide by secular criteria in hiring and firing. Ball said he did not really think there was a concerted effort on the part of the Court to secularize the society.

Responding to a request from Richard Neuhaus to name the six Supreme Court justices who could probably be counted on to oppose public aid to religious schools, Ball took as his barometer *Meek* v. *Pittenger,* a 1973 case wherein the Court struck down programs to provide auxiliary services and to loan instructional equipment to religious schools. Justice Stewart wrote the majority opinion in that decision. He was joined by Justices Blackmun, Powell, Brennan, and Marshall. Justice Stevens, who did not vote, could probably be counted on that side. Dissenting were Chief Justice Burger and Justices White and Rehnquist.

Ball speculated that three cases dealing with this general aid area could come before the Supreme Court in the next few years. One would be the tax credit case, if the legislation is enacted. Another would be a Pennsylvania case involving the busing of children to a religious school. The third case would involve the Elementary and Secondary Education Act as applied to religious schools across the country. A test case is in the federal court system in New York. Ball did not want to venture a guess on how these cases would turn out.

Richard Morgan's Overview

In looking for forces that have created an atmosphere for the Supreme Court decision against aid to private schools, Richard Morgan suggested an investigation of the Harvard Law School's influence on the Court. He then raised two objections to Ball's paper. His first objection was to Ball's stress upon the "free exercise" clause to protect religious liberties. Morgan would prefer an argument for protection based in the "freedom of speech and association" clause. Otherwise, religious schools would be carving out a separate, and unfortunate, exemption in public law for themselves.

Morgan's second objection was to Ball's theory that the free exercise clause places a positive obligation on government to enable parents to afford the option of a religious education for their children. Morgan found this argument weaker than the non-discrimination argument. If the Congress decided that providing tax credits was wise public policy, it would be an invidious discrimination to exclude from the program those who chose a church-related school.

Ball agreed readily with Morgan's first point. He himself, he noted, has argued cases not involving religious groups in which he did not rely upon the "free exercise" clause. "I believe," said Ball, "that under the cover of a decision like *Whisner,* the nonsectarian private school is beautifully protected." On the second point, Ball tried the nondiscrimination argument in a brief filed with the Supreme Court in the case of *Lemon* v. *Sloan,* but Justice Powell called the argument "spurious" in his written opinion. "I believe it's a perfectly valid argument, and I wish the Court would listen to it," Ball said.

Putting the State to the Test

Albert Huegli underscored Ball's statement that mediating structures must put the state to the test, not vice-versa. Huegli predicted that opportunities for such tests would come more and more frequently as the government attempts to control the mediating structures. Huegli's case in point was his own Valparaiso University, a small (4,500 students) church-related institution. An extraordinary number of regulatory agencies have tried to carry out "what they think is the legislation pertaining to institutions such as Valparaiso," Huegli said. "The problems that we face are less with the legislation than with the regulation. I have had a person sit across the table from me and simply say, 'We're going to make an example of you and of Notre Dame.' "

From Huegli's perspective, principles established by Supreme Court decisions are a matter quite apart from the day-to-day harassment visited upon mediating structures by regulators. The confiscatory nature of the tax structure, for example, makes it difficult to resist the IRS and the rules it wants to enforce. Huegli asked how such mediating structures can be kept viable in an age in which not just government legislation is involved, or the courts, but "the interpretation of regulations by those who may or may not be authorized under the legislation to do what they are doing."

Ball then gave the most activist advice of the conference. There is no doubt, he said, that regulators make subjective decisions under the umbrella of a statute. When regulators act in a way not authorized by the law, they must be challenged.

> The first round of a challenge is providing a legal opinion and, possibly, having a confrontation with the public servant in question. I believe that right now, for example, fundamentalists all over the country are gearing up to oppose the imposition of a definition of religion contained in the unemployment compensation policy of the U.S. government as promulgated not by Congress but by the Secretary of Labor. The Secretary of Labor has said that if you work for a religious school you are not working for a church, you are not working for an organization which exists primarily for religious purposes, you are not working for an organization that is supervised by or controlled by a religious organization; he is saying, instead, that you are working for a thing called a school. And schools are covered by Department of Labor regulations. There is a very serious question, here, of defining the mission of the church through Secretary Marshall's own prescriptions.

The fundamentalists are resisting this definition, daring the government to come after them, Ball said. "I wish other religious bodies would do the same thing."

The second round in challenging a regulator, Ball continued, is to present a clear legal position which suggests that the government might lose in court. The third round is to take the government to court and there challenge the application of the regulation "either as being not authorized by government statute or, if being authorized, as unconstitutional." These are tough actions to take, Ball acknowledged, because nobody likes to take on the government alone. Challenges cost money, and the civil servants get hostile. But if an institution such as Valparaiso University would take the lead, it would be surprised how many others would join, Ball predicted.

> The thing that bothers me is this, I think we're getting a really Prussianized mentality. I think we're feeling that we've got to live by sufferance. Secretary Marshall is a public servant. He's

not Reichsmarschal. We ought to get away from the extreme sense of caution about these people, a sense of subservience.

Richard Neuhaus said Ball had issued exactly the kind of challenge he had hoped might emerge from the conference.

The Kurland Rule

In *To Empower People,* Berger and Neuhaus appeal for a wider acceptance of the so-called Kurland Rule in the formulation of public policy. That rule, or theory, named for Philip Kurland of the University of Chicago, holds that "if a policy furthers a legitimate secular purpose it is a matter of legal indifference whether or not that policy employs religious institutions" (*To Empower People,* p. 29).

Knowing that Dean Kelley dislikes the Kurland Rule and that Richard Morgan likes it, Neuhaus asked Ball to express his opinion on it. Ball, in turn, asked Kelley to explain his objection. Kelley replied that the rule bothers him because government tends to benefit religions in some ways and not in others, thereby muddling the issue of what religions are.

William Ball's position on the Kurland Rule turned out to be close to Kelley's. "The Kurland view does not really recognize religion for what it is," he stated.

"But is there no strategic value in the Kurland Rule?" Neuhaus asked.

"Strategy for what?" Ball replied.

"For getting the Court out of the present mare's nest with regard to the definition of religion," said Neuhaus. Why not use the Kurland Rule as a persuasive argument in favor of mediating structures? "The Kurland Rule seems so sane and sensible to the non-lawyer," Berger added.

Joseph Sullivan asked Ball for more details on his defense in cases in which the National Labor Relations Board has intervened in religious schools.

The key to the cases in question, Ball explained, is that religious schools claim exemption from NLRB regulations while the federal agency claims these schools are "only partly religious." So the NLRB goes into a Catholic school, for example, and intervenes on behalf of a teacher fired for holding views contrary to the doctrines of the church.

Berger observed that this is a Catch-22 situation for the schools. They are called "totally religious" when the state does not want to give them subsidies, and "partly secular" when the state wants to regulate them.

Sullivan and Ball agreed that we must not confuse this issue with the queen's shilling issue discussed the previous day. What is at stake in the NLRB cases is no less than the definition of "religious institutions" and their legitimate exemptions from government control.

This reminded Christa Klein of the theme that seemed to be emerging earlier in the discussion, namely, the supineness of administrators of mediating structures in the face of government regulations and regulators. Again drawing on her research on American Protestant seminaries, Klein called attention to the feeling of "double jeopardy" experienced by seminarians, who have one foot in Jerusalem and one in Athens. Administrators of seminaries experience the tension too, so that when they are left to their own self-regulation they tend to accept secular definitions of their institution and mission, Klein reported. They try to prove themselves and their schools to secular society by accepting society's view of them. Therefore, the supineness when confronted with government regulations is not simply a lack of courage but is also a result of internal tensions.

Berger avoided making a summary of the discussion beyond saying that the total effect was cheering, despite some depressing evidence. He saw in the session a call-to-arms for those who care about mediating structures.

Donald Erickson's Summary

Donald Erickson's paper was the fourth and last of the conference. Richard Neuhaus had observed how irresistibly the discussion of church-state relations gravitates to the subject of schooling, and Erickson was a scholar who knew about all sorts of schools. He said we might better understand his paper if he gave us some insights into the work he has done and the experience he has had in visiting various kinds of schools. He proceeded with an anecdotal chronicle of his research on private and public schools. Erickson said he believed, for example, that "magic" is taking place in urban religious schools—the achievement scores show it. He told of his first experience with an Amish school in Iowa. It was a one-room school in simple surroundings, with a teacher who had not even been to high school. "As I was visiting that classroom, trying to understand what was going on, I sensed a remarkable lack of tension, a lack of anxiety, a remarkable oneness in the room," Erickson said. He later took a University of Chicago graduate seminar to several Amish schools, and all of the students came away with the same impression he had of the Iowa school. None of the visitors understood exactly what was going on in those schools, he stated, but they agreed that something different, something profound was happening in those "unsophisticated schools."

If, in contrast to public schools, private schools really are doing something different, why not study that "something different?" Erickson said he asked himself that question, then embarked on a research project to test some of his hunches on the nature of the difference. He found the perfect site, Canada, where Catholic schools vary a great deal according to the province they are in. In some Canadian provinces, parochial schools are totally on their own, getting no public funds. In others, Catholic schools get approximately the same amount of public money as public schools. And still other provinces have other patterns.

Erickson's research in Canada is still underway, but he shared some of the preliminary findings. For example, the data indicate that the crucial element in the quality of alternative schooling is the presence of choice, not simply money. Parents and teachers think a publicly supported Catholic school is better if there is a choice between that school and an equally supported secular public school.

The next phase of the research, Erickson explained, is to look at the effects of the newly passed modified voucher system in Canada.

> We want to study the impact of public aid upon independent schools, as they are called there; we want to study the impact of the new competition upon the public schools; we want to study the effects of a voucher system upon parental choice, and we want to look at the consequences of this program for political conflict.

Erickson then referred to the lengthy treatment in his paper of the influence of "institutional jeopardy" upon the commitment of teachers, students, and parents to a private school. One key research question in the Canadian study is: What happens to the *Gemeinschaft* in private schools if public money takes away their sense of institutional jeopardy? What, in short, are the effects of public money upon all the variables in Figure 4 in Erickson's paper?

Erickson said he is amazed at the degree to which the literature on schools assumes that technical competence is the goal of school. The literature on such things as student motivation and teacher commitment is very thin. Some of the most influential educational research over the past few years has assumed that "length of exposure to instruction" is a fair measure of a learning process without taking into account student commitment to the goal of the instruction. This is a pressing research question:

> What is more determinative of what happens in the classroom—the technical competence of the teacher, the kind of learning experiences of the child, the acquaintance of the child with that material, or the ability of the child in skills essential to learning the material? Or is it possible that we have been looking at secondary determinants of learning, and that perhaps the really powerful determinants are the things that we see in the Amish farm school and in some inner-city Catholic schools?

The term "motivation," Erickson said, inadequately describes the quality he is trying to isolate. He prefers "commitment," a term he felt he must define more clearly than he did in his paper. He defined "commitment" in terms of relationships:

> Children in these schools learn a particular subject matter not only because it is inherently interesting but because of the relationship between the child and the teacher, and the relationship between the child and the parents, because of the norm of reciprocity that seems to prevade the whole place.
>
> What the state is doing, I am afraid, in some of its regulations is trying to impose upon the *Gemeinschaft* institutions so many *Gesellschaft* standards—technical competence, coldly calculated—that it is going to stamp out the very things that makes these schools work.

In concluding his summary remarks, Erickson returned to his greatest concern, namely, the debilitating effects of money, even "the smell of money," upon the special complex of factors that make up people's commitment to private schools. He fears that the expectation of "payment" thwarts commitment. "One of the most rewarding experiences available to man," he said, "is an experience of doing something without getting a financial reward, just doing it because you feel that your efforts make a big difference. I think we're forgetting that."

Minimalist and Maximalist

David Seeley initiated the discussion by volunteering the information that research by his organization, the Public Education Association, has come to almost the identical conclusions as Erickson's. That is, what he calls the "productive learning relationship" is the key factor in schooling. Seeley and Erickson agreed that the relationship between commitment and money is a fragile one that we do not completely understand.

Peter Berger stepped in to ground the discussion in the terms of the mediating structures project.

> As you know, this project has had two hypotheses—the maximalist and the minimalists hypotheses—that we have been exploring and testing. My own thinking on this increasingly tends toward the idea that the minimalist hypothesis will be strengthened, that maybe our maximalist hypothesis was a mistake. What we are talking about this afternoon is absolutely crucial to that question. What happens if mediating structures, in this case religious ones, take government money? Now, here's my simplification of our discussion so far. I'm not sure how Father Coleman's paper fits into all this, but the other three come out

with a resounding no to government money. Dean Kelly tells us no because it would corrupt religion. Mr. Ball tells us no because the Supreme Court won't allow it, and I think that Professor Erickson is telling us no because it would corrupt education. May I ask this: If, for the moment, we were to bracket the legal question, can we think of some mechanism by which the corrupting effects of government money might be avoided?

A flurry of responses offered not new mechanisms for avoiding the corrupting effects of government money but new wrinkles to the problem. Albert Huegli, for example, blamed the confiscatory nature of the tax system for the problems of private schools. With private wealth gone, he said, more and more private institutions must go to the government well. John Eagan, who chairs the housing panel of the Mediating Structures Project, reminded us that one object of the project is to discover the connections between mediating structures so that they do not stand alone. Ellen Idler, who works with the health care panel, addressed the "professional bias" of the participants around the table. She stressed the importance of lay resources.

The discussion was clearly not addressing Berger's call for new mechanisms for taking government money while resisting co-optation. Finally, Erickson offered a suggestion.

I am constantly astonished at the power of the mystique of the "minimum standards" idea. People seem to buy the idea that somewhere there is a definition of what constitutes a good school. There really is nothing in the education research literature that defines a good school. And the people who put numbers down into columns and who issue hundreds of pages of regulations just do not know what they are talking about. Given this fact, wouldn't it be better not to cast the present system into the concrete of eternity? Wouldn't it be better to try a lot of different things? Let's let the Tabernacle Christian School try the Accelerated Christian Education material, let's let some other little school try something entirely different. If the state is entitled to demand anything at all, then it should be able to specify what it is entitled to demand. Why don't we simply measure the end product of schools and not worry about what happens in schools as long as what happens is not destructive to the health of kids and the psyches of teachers?

Ted Kerrine, executive director of the Mediating Structures Project, asked Erickson to comment upon the Alum Rock California experiment with the voucher system. Erickson briefly described the Alum Rock school district's aborted experiment, one that was not, he said, a true test of the voucher idea because of the many compromises that doomed it from the start. Most importantly, the experiment failed to empower parents to make free choices about their children's schooling. It became simply a decentralization scheme, one that didn't work. "I explain all this in terms of 'Erickson's Rubber Duck Model of Innovation in Education.' My hypothesis is that schools are extraordinarily able to twist themselves into all kinds of shapes in order to get money, as if they were a rubber duck. But the moment the money and the pressure are released, they resume the old shape."

As before, Joseph Sullivan seemed less wary of government funding than were others at the table, and he responded to Berger's challenge (to find mechanisms that avoid the corrupting power of government) to make a short speech about his philosophy of the relationship between funding and commitment. Leadership and the articulate expression of an organization's mission, Sullivan said, are two important ways to exact commitment from the workers in a public service organization.

> While we, the Catholic charities, have all kinds of government funding sources, I have never seen in the tactical arena a lessening of commitment on the part of our people because they feel there is a purpose to which they are about, a purpose very different from their government counterparts. There is, for example, no philosophy in the city hospital system.

An institutional philosophy means commitment, and the poor who are served by these institutions must see commitment, he said, continuing: "If a sectarian mediating structure loses its capacity to be an advocate, then it has been co-opted. If it is no longer willing to stand up and fight just because it might lose a contract, then it has become demoralized and has lost its identity." Service and commitment are indispensable parts of the meaning of a religious institution, Sullivan concluded; "A liturgy that does not relate to life is, to me, a vacuous liturgy. If it doesn't celebrate the pain and the hurt as well as the successes and joys of the community, then it is not a real liturgy."

Berger pursued his earlier question: How can we take government money without being corrupted? It is all well and good to talk about commitment and *Gemeinschaft,* he said, but when all is said and done, money is needed to operate a mediating structure.

Perhaps, David Seeley said, an institutional strategy for taking money without compromising standards lies in Erickson's simple suggestion that schools and agencies rely on achievement tests as the final measure of whether a school is doing its job. Seeley put this in the form of a question about the standards the state might have a legitimate right to impose. If some of the legitimate state interests regarding socialization in general can be laid out on the table, then some testing system might, with minimal interference, satisfy the state that its legitimate interests have been served by a school. "There are," Seeley said, "some ground rules in a pluralistic society." He thought it would be helpful to specify, especially in the area of values, where the state has a compelling interest in intervening in the socialization process.

William Ball expressed doubt that there is an advantage in having an official definition of "compelling state interest." "If you want a pluralistic society, then don't have it under a governmental umbrella that tells you just how you shall be pluralistic," he said. Ball would put his faith not in objective, minimal standards but in the wisdom and common sense of judges who rule on cases as they come up.

Sullivan had a different, institutional/structural strategy to offer in response to Berger. "Mediating structures will have to change themselves. That is, they will have to maximize the opportunity for the participation of their members and of the people they serve."

Erickson endorsed this assertion, warning against the conclusion that members of a mediating structure lose all their commitment just because they lose their sense of institutional jeopardy. "If a sense of special mission is strong enough," he said, "it can override the need for a sense of jeopardy." The *Gemeinschaft* type of mediating structure is less an absolute type than a range along a scale of several gradations of commitment to an institution.

Connecting the Strands

Neuhaus tried to tie together some of the strands of the discussion.

> To the question Peter Berger poses, I wonder if there aren't three mechanisms we have been talking about. One is simply legal, and that is ongoing. The legal mechanism can be pursued, as Dean Kelley would want, through the free exercise of religion clause or, as Dick Morgan would want, through the more general freedom of speech approach.
>
> The second mechanism, one we've slighted a bit, is structural, one in which we redefine the enterprise (education, health care, and the like) so radically that the mediating structure, in its new shape, will not be as susceptible to the intrusion of the state as it was in its old form. The third is also a structural mechanism, one that I hope we'll pursue more. This mechanism involves building as many steps as possible between the funding source, the queen, and where her shilling goes. Education vouchers are one example of this mechanism.

Berger accepted Neuhaus's first and third mechanisms as responses relevant to his question, but he said the second does not involve the taking of government money. Neuhaus argued that the second point has relevance. Redefining education, he suggested, might be a good way to lessen the risk of government intervention after receiving public money.

David Seeley wanted the group to return to his agenda—accountability. It is appropriate, he said, to imagine mechanisms for the protection of mediating structures, but there still must be accountability to the public. There have to be standards that meet the legitimate, compelling interests of the state. What are the least dangerous ways of satisfying those interests? Erickson was intrigued with Seeley's formulation and joined in asking the rest of us to try to specify what the state has the right to demand for every child from every school.

One formula that embodies the seemingly legitimate public concern is the Supreme Court's criterion of "clear and present danger to the public health and safety," Dean Kelley offered. Another accepted area of legitimate public concern involves protection against chicanery and fraud, he said, adding his suspicion of laws meant to protect us from our own less virtuous qualities. Kelley was not sure chicanery and fraud constitute a legitimate state interest.

Erickson suggested that we explore the question in another way. Let's ask: "What are the utter prerequisites of good citizenship?"

Peter Skerry, a researcher with the Mediating Structures Project, noted the failure of the New Jersey Department of Education to come up with precisely those criteria. I suggested that the list of qualities for being a good citizen might be minimal. Perhaps it is sufficient to ask only that the child learn to read a newspaper; if the freedom of the press is guaranteed and defended in another sector, then perhaps the ability to read a newspaper meets the minimal legitimate state interests. People do not have to be nice, and they do not necessarily have to like one another for a culture to operate. Social scientists are tending less and less to look at culture as (in anthropologist Anthony Wallace's terms) "the replication of uniformity" and more and more as "the organization of diversity."

Neuhaus refocused attention on accountability versus state interest in education.

> Why not ask what people want for their children? The assumption is that nobody is as concerned about the education of children as their parents. I imagine that most parents want some sort of education that will keep their children out of jail, that will equip them to get a good job, and that will help them establish the kind of family life in adulthood that would have continuity with the parents' standards and values. Those are the things that parents want for their children. Imagine getting rid of compulsory school laws and leaving educational decisions entirely to the family. The state has a legitimate interest in the

health and diet of children, yet it does not have compulsory diet laws for the family. As with the diet, why not remove education from intervention, supervision, and definition of government?

Neuhaus's suggestion evoked a brief debate about the political feasibility of such an approach, and whether parents willingly surrender their powers to professionals. To the discussion, Neuhaus said that a fourth mechanism might be added to the three mechanisms for taking government money without being controlled by government, something we might call "the accountability of results rather than the accountability of process." The more we move in that direction, he said, the more protection we have.

I added that Sullivan's idea of increased participation by the members of a mediating structure may be a fifth mechanism of protection.

Berger interpreted Father Sullivan's point as having to do with political clout, participation involving political mobilization.

John Egan declared that whatever the mechanisms are for empowering people, the key concept is hope. Without hope, education and the chance of getting a job will mean little in the lives of the people.

Neuhaus asked if there were any summary statements.

"Certainly not *a* summary statement," said Berger. "I think we can all agree with Jack Egan that there is hope, but I think it would be inappropriate to end this conference on a note of reassurance."

Summing Up: Is There a New Shape to the Church-State Debate?

The preceding chapters chronicle the give-and-take of a two-day conference on "The New Shape of the Church-State Debate." In the discussion there was an underlying pattern of themes and counterthemes which emerged slowly as each of the four papers added to one continuing conversation. It is now appropriate to ask: What is the shape of the church-state debate as it emerged at the conference and in what way can it be called "new"?

There were many elements of the old frame for posing church-state questions. Several classic lines were visible early in the proceedings, such as when the queen's shilling metaphor caught our imagination. During that part of the conference, the participants seemed to be establishing their positions on subsidy and control. The positions of Dean Kelley and Richard Morgan were illuminated as they disagreed on the concept of "extraterritoriality." James Wood and James Dunn set forth the "strict separationist" view. In contrast, Joseph Sullivan and Arthur Hertzberg preferred—for different reasons, I think—the maximalist strategy in which government takes an active role in empowering mediating structures and making them accountable. There was a similar division of the house regarding the prophetic role of the churches in contributing moral wisdom and content to public policy decisions. Dean Kelley and James Wood steadfastly insisted that the churches could be prophetic only if they are protected from both state subsidy and state control. Sullivan and a few others thought that the churches could be prophetic only insofar as they are involved in the everyday lives of people, and that involvement, Sullivan thought, might legitimately involve what Kelley would consider "entanglement" with government.

These early, bipolar positions, however, do not adequately reflect the complexity of the issues as they emerged during the conference. There is a sense in which the central theme of the entire event was *power,* despite the fact that the term was used rarely. The goal of the mediating structures project is, after all, "empowerment"—the empowering of people and their "people-sized" institutions. Moreover, the discussion was frequently about the *balance of power* between the mediating structures (specifically religious) and the state. Most participants refused to accept Arthur Hertzberg's dichotomous question, "Do we put our trust in the government or in the mediating structures?" Rather, most people seemed to want to articulate the complexities inherent in a balance between the state and mediating structures. One tacit assumption was that American democratic pluralism works best when there is a creative tension between healthy, powerful mediating structures on the one hand and a healthy, powerful, but self-restrained, state on the other.

Mediating structures derive their natural power from their *Gemeinschaft* qualities, from their function as generators of morality. The state derives its natural authority from the collective decision that certain public interests transcend individual rights. *Gemeinschaft* and morality, unfortunately, are not sufficient to maintain the power of mediating structures in the public sphere today. The health and power of mediating structures was a major concern at the conference. As Peter Berger put it, cash is needed to do things. Cash is power of a kind; parents are empowered by giving them cash to make decisions about the schooling and health care of their children. Mediating structures are empowered by giving them cash, or not seizing their cash, so they can perform social services of legitimate public interest. Mediating structures are also given power to the extent that the state restrains its police and regulatory powers. Many of the issues raised at the conference swirled around this fundamental question: What constitutes a proper and healthy balance between the mediating structures of religion and the state?

The search for a formula for achieving the balance of power always led back to three related issues—professionalization, accountability, and justice. These are closely related because they represent different approaches to the same question. Dean Kelley asked, "What is the meaning of individual freedom in the context of community rights?" Later Richard Neuhaus pleaded for a return to that issue: "At what point do the faith rights that are claimed come into conflict with the legitimate rights of the community?" To speak of rights and freedom in the context of American pluralism is to speak of responsibility, and responsibility involves accountability. And to speak of rights and responsibilities in, say, the specific case of a school that teaches racism or anti-Semitism leads inevitably to considerations of justice. Thus are these three issues—professionalization, accountability, and justice—intertwined in ways that resist separation.

Every time one of the three issues came up at the conference the other two were sure to follow. Take professionalization, for example. In *To Empower People,* Berger and Neuhaus announced their skepticism of the professionalization of social services within mediating structures. Many persons at the conference picked up this theme. Professionalization has a *Gesellschaft* quality that threatens the natural power of the mediating

116

structures. As Christa Klein put it, workers in mediating structures, be they clergy or teachers or physicians, endure intense role conflict as they increasingly define themselves as "professionals." Accountability follows from that: Klein said that one tendency of professionals is to become accountable only to other professionals, instead of to the public they serve.

Berger had other "worries" about professionalization and accountability: a worry about religio-ethnic gangsterism within mediating structures, a worry that professional bureaucrats in government will attack mediating structures, a worry that the nonprofessionals within and without the mediating structures will surrender their decision-making power to professionals. Hertzberg's question about where to put trust, in the state or in mediating structures, is a dilemma of accountability.

Into the professionalization-accountability mix comes justice. Hertzberg asked, "How can I keep such-and-such a school from teaching anti-Semitism?" That question cuts right to the heart of the conflict between faith rights and community rights. It appeared that our best chance for making a clear distinction about individual rights versus community rights was to focus upon the concrete example of a Christian fundamentalist school. If that school does not get direct public subsidies (bracketing the question of whether tax credits are subsidies), what may the state legitimately, in the public interest, ask the school to do?

The conference participants had no clear consensus on the range of pluralism, the sort of "kookiness," tolerable in the public interest. Recent events such as efforts of Nazis to march in Skokie, Illinois, haunted the discussion of anti-Semitism in the schools. And Berger and Neuhaus admitted they had no clear justification for treating racism as the only exception to their axiom: "Discrimination is the essence of particularism, and particularism is the essense of pluralism."

The conference quickly abandoned any attempt to agree upon the values it is in the public interest to teach in schools. It moved to the more neutral criterion of skills, but fared no better there. Most people finally agreed with Donald Erickson's suggestion that the state might measure the end product of all schools, allowing a diversity of educational approaches without trying to control the process. Neuhaus dubbed this "the accountability of results, not of process," but agreement with even this conclusion was neither unanimous nor enthusiastic.

The attempt to balance the power of the state and the power of mediating structures, and the strain of needing to deal simultaneously with professionalization, accountability, and justice, persisted. Berger's challenge to image mechanisms for accepting government money (and the power it buys) while avoiding the corrupting effects brought the discussion full circle—back to Dean Kelley's queen's shilling metaphor. In the course of the exercise in inventing legal and structural mechanisms for resisting external control and internal corruption, there was always a "but." *But* what about accountability to the members of the mediating structure? *But* what about accountability to the public? *But* what about the legitimate interests of the state in controlling the destructive and divisive potential lurking in mediating structures? Clearly, we were talking about so delicate a balance between the powers and responsibilities of mediating structures and those of the state that any counter placed on one side of the scale evoked a worried response from the other side.

Should an indecisive conclusion be used to declare the conference a failure? I think not. The tensions and contradictions of the conference dramatized the dilemmas and paradoxes inherent in the fragile contract that is American culture. To say there must be a creative tension between healthy, functioning mediating structures on the one hand and a responsible, self-restraining state on the other is, of course, much easier than making the tension work. But naming the tension, if only to remind ourselves that this is a natural state of affairs, is an important exercise.

I saw in the conference a theme that may bypass the deadlocks that stymie the church-state debates. Father John Coleman anticipated that theme when he tried to make the group see that many of the "problems" being raised were *church* problems, not church-state problems, but the emotional peak of the conference was the session devoted to William Ball's paper and presentation. The message brought by Ball was that mediating structures should see what they can do for themselves. They are their own enemy when they lack courage to resist government controls. Supineness in the face of government regulators, kowtowing to professionals, failing to insure maximum participation of members within mediating structures—these are the church problems which can be met apart from the legal battles of church-state tensions.

As Peter Berger and Richard Neuhaus both conceded, the momentum of the conference seemed to be in favor of the minimalist proposition that "public policy should protect and foster mediating structures." Ball's challenge was consistent with this proposition, as was Berger's challenge to imagine strategies for resisting both control and corruption. On the basis of the human intensity of these challenges alone, I would say that the conference discovered a new shape to an old question.

Lest these comments sound too reassuring and approving, I should add a few observations on a troubling fact about the makeup of the final group of participants. It is true that the conference assembled some of the most important thinkers on the church-state question, but there were notable gaps in what otherwise would have been a representative group. The fact that the second day was Saturday meant there were no identifiably Jewish responses to Ball's and Erickson's papers. Also, although people such as Babette Edwards of the Harlem Parents Union and Jesse

Jackson of Operation PUSH were invited, they could not attend, and there were no black, brown, red, or yellow faces around the table. I felt a bit uncomfortable as we began to talk about the sort of schooling the poor want for their children: How could we be sure we were not projecting onto poor parents the middle-class values of what was, to be sure, a group of white professionals? The answer was, we could not. Having present persons who work with the poor was not the same as listening to persuasive spokespersons for the wants and dreams of the poor.

What, if any, impact will the conference have on the church-state debate? At the very least, all four authors of conference papers found in the mediating structures idea an exciting handle for understanding their own special work on church-state problems. *To Empower People* inspired William Ball and apparently provided Donald Erickson with some terms useful in the research he is doing. The participants, if still uncertain about the scope of church-state questions, carried away a challenge to be more deliberate and more sensitive in specifying what the debate is about.

To name the tensions is as important as work on the details if creative tensions are the goal. If the conference and its proceedings contribute to the naming of contradictions inherent in American civilization, positive impact can be recorded.

SELECTED AEI PUBLICATIONS

Public Opinion, published bimonthly (one year, $12; two years, $22; single copy, $2.50)

A Conversation with Mayor Marion Barry (18 pp., $1.75)

A Conversation with Anne de Lattre: Developing the Sahel (19 pp., $1.75)

A Conversation with Ernesto Mulato: The Political and Military Struggle in Angola (23 pp., $1.75)

Capitalism and Socialism: A Theological Inquiry, Michael Novak, ed. (193 pp., paper $4.75, cloth $10.75)

The Past and Future of Presidential Debates, Austin Ranney, ed. (226 pp., $5.75)

The Islamic Doctrine of Economics and Contemporary Economic Thought, Muhammad Abdul-Rauf (23 pp., $2)

A Conversation with Secretary Ray Marshall: Inflation, Unemployment, and the Minimum Wage (27 pp., $2.25)

Referendums: A Comparative Study of Practice and Theory, David Butler and Austin Ranney, eds. (250 pp., $4.75)

The American Vision: An Essay on the Future of Democratic Capitalism, Michael Novak (60 pp., $2.75)

Unsafe at Any Margin: Interpreting Congressional Elections, Thomas E. Mann (116 pp., $3.25)

The New American Political System, Anthony King, ed. (407 pp., $6.75)

AEI ASSOCIATES PROGRAM

The American Enterprise Institute invites your participation in the competition of ideas through its AEI Associates Program. This program has two objectives:

The first is to broaden the distribution of AEI studies, conferences, forums, and reviews, and thereby to extend public familiarity with the issues. AEI Associates receive regular information on AEI research and programs, and they can order publications and cassettes at a savings.

The second objective is to increase the research activity of the American Enterprise Institute and the dissemination of its published materials to policy makers, the academic community, journalists, and others who help shape public attitudes. Your contribution, which in most cases is partly tax deductible, will help ensure that decision makers have the benefit of scholarly research on the practical options to be considered before programs are formulated. The issues studied by AEI include:

- Defense Policy
- Economic Policy
- Energy Policy
- Foreign Policy
- Government Regulation
- Health Policy
- Legal Policy
- Political and Social Processes
- Social Security and Retirement Policy
- Tax Policy

For more information, write to:

AMERICAN ENTERPRISE INSTITUTE
1150 Seventeenth Street, N.W.
Washington, D.C. 20036